GENE KELLY

A Celebration

GENE KELLY

A Celebration

FOREWORD BY LESLIE CARON

SHERIDAN MORLEY AND RUTH LEON

PAVILION

For Clive, with love,
admiration and thanks
from us both.

First published in Great Britain in 1996 by
PAVILION BOOKS LIMITED
26 Upper Ground, London SE1 9PD

Copyright © 1996 Sheridan Morley and Ruth Leon
The moral right of the author has been asserted.

Art direction and design by
THE BRIDGEWATER BOOK COMPANY

A CIP catalogue record for this book is available
from the British Library.

ISBN 1 85793 848 8

Printed and bound in Spain by Bookprint

2 4 6 8 10 9 7 5 3 1

This book may be ordered by post direct from the publisher.
Please contact the Marketing Department.
But try your bookshop first.

Contents

Foreword

by

LESLIE CARON

I *first met Gene in Paris, at the time when he was set to star in* An American in Paris. *He was here to test a young French actress of some renown who had taken ballet as a girl, and I was just a young ballet dancer whom he had seen on the stage, the previous year, when I was in the very exciting company of Roland Petit.*

I met him in the Hôtel Plaza Athénée. He said to me: "I might get fired for doing this. The studio only gave me permission to test ... I know you can dance, but I want to see if you can act and how you look on the screen." This was the regime at MGM. Even Gene Kelly had to do as he was told, but the studio never intimidated him.

The Metro-Goldwyn-Mayer studio was like a town. Everyone who worked there was clocked in in the morning and clocked out at the end of the day. Unless you had suffered an injury, you were expected to work from nine to six during the rehearsal periods— longer during filming because the hour and a half spent in makeup was not counted. When filming, there were black limousines to drive the stars from A to B—the others walked. During rehearsals you all walked. The executives never walked, and you never saw them, unless there was a problem.

Gene Kelly walked, like everyone else, and he was saluted with familiarity by one and all: "Hi, Geno! How you doin'?" "Hi, Sauly, see ya!" By now he had made enough films to know all the writers, actors, directors. cameramen, makeup men and hairdressers on the lot. He was democratic and during rehearsals wore beige cotton pants, a crocodile

RIGHT *Gene Kelly the dancer, performing with Leslie Caron in* An American in Paris. ☆

sweatshirt hanging out, white socks and loafers and what was then called a beany, to cover his baldness. Until Sean Connery, every balding star wore a toupee—Gene Kelly, Fred Astaire, David Niven (who called his Aubusson). They wore them on film and at parties—which were, in fact, a sort of audition ground.

Gene was very intelligent and quick to assess the qualities and defects of his partners. There was hardly time before or during a film to correct defects, so he would make the best of his partner's qualities. He was a leader. Wherever he was, he automatically took command. He was fair and generous when mentioning, in measured tones, his approval. His disapproval was just as straightforward, and delivered in even tones which did not allow for any form of excuse. He was exacting, and his rebukes were feared. He felt responsible for me—my success or failure in the film. He guided me in front of the camera with a good deal of humor. My tendency was to hide from the camera. He would invariably say: "Lester" (that was his affectionate nickname for me—Lester de Pester), "Lester, if you want your mother to see you in the film, you had better turn this way when you speak!" He looked after my health, and when I came down with mononucleosis during the filming he defended me against the studio powers for whom every

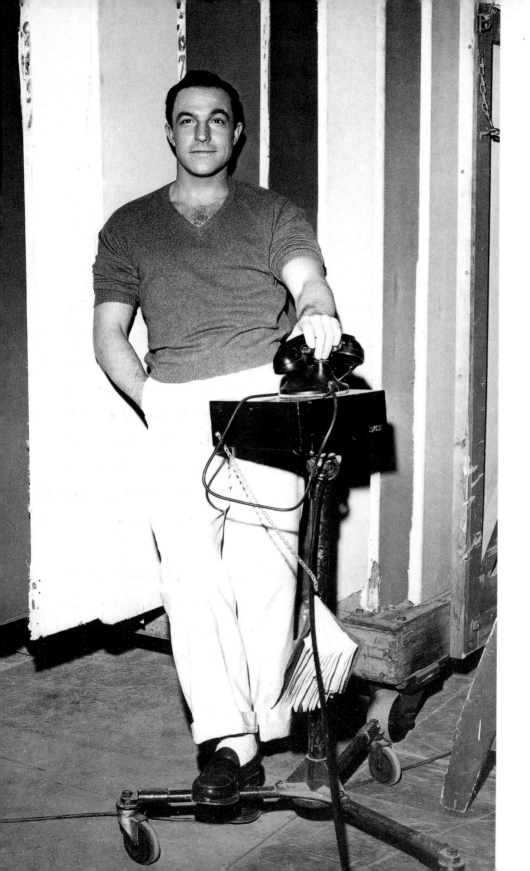

form of delay meant money. He arranged it with Production so that I would stay in bed one day and work the next. The studio doctor, Dr Brown, jabbed me every other day with B12, B complex and liver extract. He cured me in six months.

In those days, air conditioning was an unknown commodity. The sun beat with ferocious intensity on the corrugated roof of our rehearsal hall, and later, when we began shooting, the big 10 K lamps, up on the catwalks, sometimes even caused the sparks to faint and, on one or two occasions, even fall to their death. They would call from up there: "Open the doors!" Work would be interrupted, then the gaffer would yell: "Kill the broads!" which amused me because of the play on words.

During An American in Paris, *Gene played a triple part. He was not only the leading man but also the choreographer and, during the filming, directed the camera himself, which is the norm—the choreographer designs the ballets and numbers according to where he will place the camera most effectively. Gene had two assistants who worked with me during all of the rehearsals, teaching me modern dance and rehearsing me until I was feet-perfect. The first was Carol Haney, who was a great Jack Cole dancer; the other Jeanne Coyne, who had been Stanley Donen's first wife and was to be Gene's second wife. A darling girl. They were both extremely supportive. They also became Gene's alter ego when he was dancing in a scene and could not for that reason control the rest of the group.*

We worked a six-day week, so that Saturday was the night to let off steam. Gene's and Betsy Blair's front door was open—and I literally mean open. All the hoofers (the local name for dancers) would drop in after an early dinner—most of them from MGM. You went to the bar in the back of the living room, served yourself a drink and, at a certain point, a jam session would slowly take place. Anyone who felt like doing a turn did so. I saw Lena Horne sing there many times, Saul Chaplin or André Previn would play the piano, while Betsy sang out of key—but she didn't care. Carol Haney would dance, Adolph Green and Betty Comden—who were then slogging away, trying to find a plot around an impossible song, "Singin' in the Rain"—would perform a few sketches.

Gene never performed much—he didn't like his voice—but he did the Irish thing for a Saturday night: he drank his whiskey and talked. There were actors from other studios who were like familiar friends, Phil Silvers and his wife, and also visiting stars; I remember seeing Anna Magnani in a dress with the hem half undone—she didn't care either. Stanley Donen was always there, sleeping peacefully on one of the couches, amid the din. Vincente Minnelli and his wife Judy Garland, Arthur Freed, Saul Chaplin, Gene, Betsy and myself were all invited to Ira Gershwin's house for Judy's birthday. After dinner she got up and said: "This is my birthday, I'm going to sing as much as I want to." She sang for hours, looking tenderly into Vinc's eyes.

The film took eight months to rehearse and shoot. The gossip around the studio was that Gene had gone crazy designing a twenty-minute ballet—the whole of Gershwin's piece named "An American in Paris"—just near the end of the film. I think that Arthur Freed, the producer, gave him free reign, and I think it was Vincente Minnelli's idea to do the different segments in the style of his favorite painters. But, once again, Gene was laying his reputation on the line. Every time I see the film I marvel at his fabulous use of space, his knowledge of the camera and his step inventions.

In those days there were railroad tracks—a sort of tram, I guess—that took you directly from the studio in Culver City to downtown Los Angeles. All the executives and the makers of the film boarded the train and we went downtown to see the sneak

ABOVE *Gene Kelly the private man.* ☆

RIGHT *Gene Kelly the perfectionist. Leslie Caron describes him as fair, generous, but direct. "He was exacting, and his rebukes were feared."* ☆

preview. After the viewing Gene came to me and asked: "Well, kiddo, how did you like it?" I answered: "Gene, I think I have the flu." He said: "You haven't got the flu, you've just seen yourself on the screen for the first time."

We remained friends ever since. My bond of friendship tightened with the years—as an adolescent you think everything is due to you, but with time and hindsight I came to be increasingly grateful. Very few young girls had the luck to meet their Gene Kelly. About a year ago I received the honor of having a new wing in the actors' retirement home named after me. Gene was invited to present me with this honor, during a charity gala. Already very ill, he came nevertheless—he had to be carried to the podium to whisper a few words in a voice that had lost all its strength. I followed him backstage, where he said: "Only for you, Lester." I knew, and he knew, that I was never to see him again.

LESLIE CARON

Paris, June 1996

1. Plenty of ginger but no Ginger

When Gene Kelly died on February 2nd, 1996, at the age of eighty-three, he hadn't put on a pair of tap-shoes for close to thirty years but the image that flashed around the world—the man with the umbrella, dancing alone in a pool of MGM light, his face upturned in a beatific smile, while buckets of MGM rain poured down on him—was instantly recognizable even to fans who hadn't been born when he hung up his shoes. But he was far from a one-role man. Over a fifty-year career, through forty-four films, Kelly blazed a trail that younger dancers and choreographers are still trying to follow.

> "Gene was the only song-and-dance man who had balls"
>
> STANLEY DONEN

He was, after all, the man who danced with a mouse in *Anchors Aweigh*; he was the man who taught French kids to sing Gershwin in *An American in Paris*; he was the man who danced his way from the Brooklyn docks to the top of the Empire State Building in *On the Town*; and he was the man who clattered down the street attached to a dustbin lid for *It's Always Fair Weather*.

RIGHT *A publicity shot for the film with which Gene will for ever be associated above all others,* Singin' in the Rain. ☆

Kelly was one of only two song-and-dance men to make it to the very top of the Hollywood ladder, and it was he alone who moved screen dancing away from the white tie and tails of the 1930s into the urban reality of downtown Anywhere, USA. As the original Pal Joey, he brought a gritty kind of realism to what had previously been a ballroom fantasy; and, above all, he revolutionized dancing on screen at just the postwar moment when Hollywood itself was first coming to grips with that new realism.

In addition to being the first modern male screen dancer he was also, of course, actor, singer, writer, producer and director. But from his earliest days in Pittsburgh he had made dances, and it is probably as a choreographer, long after the prints of his own dancing have faded, that Kelly will always be remembered. He invented a new language, not only for the body but also for the camera, that allowed him to take dance beyond what could be achieved in real time on a stage into a realm where cinema allowed him to stretch reality into a new art form. Where Fred Astaire and Ginger Rogers remained essentially stage-bound, often repeating routines which Fred had first created for Broadway and the West End, Kelly was the first to recognize what could be done by marrying technology to art. He was also the first to push those possibilities to the limit—

whether dancing with cartoons or with himself in double exposure. From *For Me and My Gal* onwards, every film was an experiment in trying to express through movement what had until then been said only in words and pictures. Although there had been dancers of all stripes since the advent of sound in the cinema, filmed dance came of age with Gene Kelly. In that sense he was the father of the modern dance explosion, combining ballet and contemporary dance techniques to produce an original style that was both acrobatic and subtle. And he did it more or less alone, certainly without a regular partner to bounce ideas off and try things out on.

It was the American novelist John Updike, writing a brilliant *New Yorker* study of Kelly a couple of years before he died, who got to the heart of it:

"He had plenty of ginger but no Ginger; although he danced affectingly with Leslie Caron, snappily with Judy Garland, bouncily with Rita Hayworth, broodily with Vera-Ellen and respectfully with statuesque, stony-faced Cyd Charisse, we still think of Gene Kelly as a guy in loafers and a tight T-shirt, tap-dancing up a storm all by his lonesome."

There were better dancers in Hollywood, certainly there were better actors and singers, but none of them combined his talents with a formidable intelligence and a single-mindedness to invent a new form of cinema the way Gene did. There was, as his friend and sidekick Stanley Donen once noted, an overwhelming, unstoppable energy which blew away all your reservations.

When Astaire is about to dance the shot changes, the music unmistakably swells and we await an interruption of real life for the duration of the routine. When Kelly dances he has moved so subtly from standing to movement to art that it looks as though anyone could do it. If Fred Astaire showed us on the screen what we dreamed of being, it was Kelly who showed us what we really could be.

There were three marriages, three children and an active social life. But there was another side too. Gene had an active social conscience that drove him to take risks with his Hollywood reputation. He was fearless in his support of what he believed in, whether it was in fashion or not. His outspoken support of such unpopular causes as religious equality dated from his college experience of being excluded from joining a fraternity because he was Catholic and his best friend was Jewish.

He and his first wife, Betsy Blair, were the originators of The Game, a highly competitive form of charades that was both enjoyed and feared by their friends. Gene did not like to lose and would sulk if his team didn't win, even in a friendly game in his own house. When his second wife, Jeanie Coyne, died, Gene refused all work that would take him away from his children and set about becoming a single parent with the same dedication and concentration which he had earlier employed to start the family dancing school in Johnstown, Pennsylvania, while getting his degree on a scholarship or playing semi-professional ice hockey in his home town.

Indoctrinated from birth with the ethos of hard work and imbued by a tough mother with boundless belief in himself, Gene always knew he'd make it in whatever field he chose to enter. What he was going to be was a lawyer, the best in Pittsburgh. Failing that, he'd be a professional sportsman. But there were many ball players in America and even more lawyers. What he finally became was unique. He became Gene Kelly.

RIGHT *In graceful motion with Cyd Charisse in the whimsical Lerner and Loewe musical* Brigadoon. ☆

2. The Mozart of the Ice Rink

Eugene Curran Kelly was the third child and second son of James and Harriet Tracy Kelly of Pittsburgh, Pennsylvania. He arrived—in an appropriate hurry—on August 3rd, 1912 to join a "lace-curtain" Irish family of some means, at least by comparison with other Catholic families in the neighborhood. James was a phonograph salesman, a husband and father of high moral rectitude with invincible convictions about the efficacy of hard work and regular attendance at mass, which he transferred to his son. Gene was to carry those principles with him into that bastion of Godlessness, Hollywood, where he worked harder than anyone else, ever.

> "The girls thought I was bloody marvelous, and pretty soon I began to believe them"
>
> GENE KELLY

RIGHT *The ten-year-old Gene putting on an early show with his brothers Jim (left) and Fred (right)—three of The Five Kellys.* ☆

Harriet was formidable, one of that generation of women who, as the daughters of immigrants, had themselves experienced the discrimination routinely doled out to foreigners. These women ruled their families with a steel will and an icy determination that their children would participate in the American dream that had so often eluded their fathers. They believed with all their hearts that, with enough effort and education, their sons would grow up to be Presidents of the United States. They were American born and they had their rights. And whenever Gene forgot any of that, his mother was there to remind him. (Eugene naturally became Gene when he started high school, although he didn't care for the abbreviation, believing it to be a girl's name.) Right up until he went to New York for his first Broadway show Harriet was mother, friend, guide, business partner and conscience, and her influence was immeasurable throughout his life.

Already in residence at the house on the corner of Portland and Bryant Streets in the Highland Park section of Pittsburgh were Gene's elder sister Harriet (always known as Jay) and his brother James. It was a pleasant, sunny house (whenever there *was* any sun in Pittsburgh, which wasn't often) and the family was happy there until Gene was two and they moved to larger quarters to await the birth of his younger sister, Louise, and his baby brother, Fred. To get the space they needed they had to move downmarket to a blue-collar street which, according to Gene, was as close to a slum as a respectable neighborhood could be. Although James was by now the top traveling salesman for the Columbia Phonograph Company, he had seven mouths to feed, and Mellon Street in the East Liberty section of town was what he could afford. There was always food on the table and clothes on their backs but Eugene and his brothers and sisters knew that it was a struggle for Harriet to make ends meet and, as they grew up, they helped in whatever way they could with afterschool jobs and extracurricular moneymaking activities

James was away all week selling his records and phonographs. He never learned to drive and had to drag his samples all over his territory on the train. But he always came home to Harriet and the children on Fridays, when she dressed them in Buster Brown suits and pretty dresses and marched them to the station to welcome him back. Weekends were devoted to family meals, church attendance and sport. James Kelly was a passionate sports fan and, depending on the season, would take his sons to baseball, football, basketball and boxing matches and whatever

ABOVE *The baby Gene had poise in front of the camera, but of all the brothers it was Fred for whom their mother predicted a future as a dancer.* ☆

other local athletic contests were on offer. But his special love was ice hockey and at that Gene excelled from the age of four when James put him on double runners—ice skates with two blades instead of one—and taught him everything he knew about moving fast over a slippery surface. This gave Gene a sense of balance that he never lost and, years later, in *It's Always Fair Weather*, he was able to teach himself a dance routine on roller skates that made use of all James's tips on weight transfer and body positioning. By the time he was eight Gene was the best skater in the neighborhood, a self-described "Mozart of the ice rink," and he had acquired a love for physical effort and competitive achievement that was to make him the unique dancer of his generation as well as a fanatical sports fan until the day he died.

James and Harriet had a gift for what we would today call parenting. All the Kelly children have talked of the security of their childhoods; their sense of knowing who they were and how they fitted into their family, their neighborhood, their school, their city and their country. Holidays, from Christmas to the Fourth of July were celebrated joyously and with much family-based homemade partying. Birthdays and St Valentine's Days were given great importance and Harriet's trade-mark thrift was put into abeyance for the day.

The summers of Gene's childhood were particularly happy. Harriet, knowing that life was less expensive in the country and intelligent enough to know that not much work gets done in the last fortnight before a vacation or the first one of a new school year, took them all out of class and out of grimy industrial Pittsburgh at the first possible moment. She found them a rented cottage in the Pennsylvania hills. Here they could spend all day out of doors, swimming, riding, canoeing on the lake, going for nature walks with James at the weekends, fishing and helping the local farmers. Clothes were limited to swimsuits and shorts.

Gene loved every minute, not least because of the relaxation of the family dress code. There were few rebellions against his parents' teachings—a brief anti-religious phase in high school was one—but a trait Gene never inherited from James was his father's love of elegance and his belief that a man should be formally dressed at all times, even in his own home in case somebody called round unexpectedly. From the time he left home Gene was unalterably casual in his dress—"a walking slum" was how he described himself. At work in the studio, at home and even on the screen, he was dressed whenever possible in comfortable cotton trousers, a form-fitting T-shirt and sneakers.

While he was at the lake Gene met the boxer, Harry Greb, then world lightweight champion, within a local training camp, who offered to give Gene some boxing lessons. This was not just another physical skill to be mastered but also had some practical application when he returned to Pittsburgh. As a Catholic in a tough mixed neighborhood, Gene often ran foul of the local Protestant kids who thought they could beat him up because he was physically small and underdeveloped. With his bodily coordination and a few tricks from the boxer he invariably emerged triumphant and, after a few face-losing confrontations, the bullies learned to leave him alone.

But he nearly didn't survive childhood at all. The only one of all the Kelly children to be seriously ill, Gene was both somewhat sickly and accident-prone. Throughout his childhood this otherwise perfect physical specimen was always breaking limbs or joints while the others hardly had a scratch.

At the age of seven Gene contracted a virulent form of pneumonia which nearly killed him. His mother's youngest brother, Gene's Uncle Gus, suggested that his lungs would recover more quickly if he learned gymnastics. He never grew tall and was always disappointed that this militated against his being a basketball player, but there was nothing to stop him becoming a world-class gymnast. Except Harriet.

Looking back, it is remarkable that Harriet managed to prevent Gene from becoming a professional sportsman, but this she did by the far-from-simple expedient of instilling in him and in all her children a love of the arts and her own determination that they would be something special. Sport was not special enough. Law was what she had in mind for her middle child and she very nearly managed it.

Harriet had no patience with idleness and her oft-quoted homily "If you're bored, I'll find you something to do," was heard by the children as a threat. At the lake they used to put on their own plays and entertainments for the other children in the area, and Jim, Jay, and Gene would teach any child who wanted to learn how to sing, dance and recite. That way they were assured of a permanent cast to back up Fred, who was quite stagestruck from babyhood.

By the time he was eight Fred had a sideline in staging magic and puppet shows in the family's basement. This proved so successful that he expanded his repertoire into Houdini-type escapes and even, once, a dog show. Many years later Fred told Gene's biographer, Clive Hirschhorn: "Gene had very little to do with these shows. He never did like small-time showbiz, though occasionally he

RIGHT *James and Harriet Kelly with their five children. Back row (left to right): Jay, Louise. Front row: Fred, Jim, and Gene.* ☆

would agree to help out with the props. He always believed that if you couldn't do something in a big way, don't do it at all."

The Kelly children themselves had dance and music lessons from professionals as soon as they could walk. Harriet saw to that, and she kept them at it even when Jim, Gene, and Fred, who were the only boys in the dance classes, complained that they were routinely being beaten up on their way home by boys calling them sissies. These local thugs in training were inflicting so much damage on her precious boys that she agreed to send them to and from classes in a taxi, but she never let them quit. She believed that they all had God-given talent and that God had put her on earth to encourage them.

As a result, they could all dance and sing, and she formed them into a group collectively if unoriginally known as The Five Kellys, or pairs consisting of Fred and Louise, Gene and Jim, Jay and Jim or any other combination of whoever didn't have too much homework to practice—until Jim, who hated it all, grew old enough to stand up to Harriet and announce that he was hanging up his tap-shoes for ever.

By the time Gene was ten the nuns at St Raphael's had started starring him in the school shows. He would probably have enjoyed these early appearances much more if he hadn't still been being tormented by the other boys as a sissy for knowing how to tap-dance. "It was all right when I was playing football with them and being one of the gang," he later told Hirschhorn, "but when they saw me all dressed up on the stage—singing and dancing —that was a different story. And being a little guy, you can imagine how self-conscious I was."

In the meantime, in 1924 James decided he was doing well enough to buy the family's first house, albeit on a large mortgage, and they moved to a pleasant, three-storey home on Kensington Street in a middle-class neighborhood. The older children attended the state school, Peabody High, but the private academy Arnold Boys' School was close enough for Gene to avail himself of their excellent sports facilities. By now the five children were showing distinctive traits. Jim was a talented painter who fought Harriet to become a successful commercial artist. She, predictably, had wanted him to become an engineer. The arts were all very well, she thought, but they should remain a hobby for anyone less talented than Fred. Gene was, of course, going to be a brilliant lawyer and the girls were, well, girls. Louise was sweet-natured and artistic, Jay was exceptionally academically gifted, and it was she and Gene who shone at school. But Harriet recognized Fred's gift for entertaining early on and by the

time he was seven she would take him to gigs all over Pittsburgh, including honkytonks that she certainly wouldn't have attended on her own. Fred could earn up to $10 a gig and his *pièce de résistance* was an adagio dance act with a six-year-old girl who would leap into his arms off a high piano for their "big finish."

This fascination with entertainment can be dated to Harriet's frustrations. She had always been interested in the theatre and, although it was unthinkable for a well-brought-up Catholic girl to become an actress at the turn of the century, she had enjoyed appearing in amateur theater productions right up to the birth of her first child, Jay. She ensured therefore that all of her children were exposed to as many professional performances as possible, and would even take them out of school for a day if a particularly distinguished performer was coming to town. She would occasionally show off her own elocution by declaiming epic verses in the hope of engendering some interest in the spoken word, but either she was a terrible actress or her children were too active to be taken by the legitimate theatre. Instead they continued to dance, sing and play at least one musical instrument each. Gene played the violin, which he hated, and he eventually gave it up in favour of the banjo—an instrument of which, it may be assumed, Harriet

RIGHT *Another early outfit, suggesting that at least one or two of Gene's later roles were predestined.* ☆

disapproved but which was better than nothing. His mother had arranged for The Five Kellys to appear in a showcase for a local dancing school at the Nixon Theater and they had been an enormous hit.

By now in high school, Gene suddenly realized that despite his diminutive size girls were really interested in him, and not because of his sporting prowess, nor yet for his high academic achievement. No, they wanted him for his dancing and singing, his ability to entertain them. His voice, even after it broke, was high and clear and he had great presence.

Gene finally stopped pulling in the opposite direction and began enjoying the limelight, his confidence given a tremendous boost. And his social life improved dramatically. "Normally those girls wouldn't have given me a second look if I hadn't been such a hit in the school shows but the fact that I was made all the difference. Most of those girls were head and shoulders taller than me. But it made me popular and I could get almost anyone I wanted to come to the school dances with me. Some of them thought I was bloody marvelous, and pretty soon I began to believe them." Gene later said that he was terrible in the shows, but as the high-school year books recorded that he was destined to be a great entertainer, he decided that he must have had *something*.

This was perhaps the first time that he seriously considered the possibility of a professional life as a dancer. It was not, however, something he talked about at the time, probably because Harriet's ambition to make him into the first Irish Catholic Supreme Court Justice was still paramount. Jules Steinberg was a close friend who found Gene's propensity for suddenly breaking into dance while walking down the street puzzling. "I had no idea Gene was interested in dancing. I now find it strange that never, in all the time I knew Gene, did he ever mention his interest in show business to me or his desire to be a dancer. It was something he kept absolutely secret until he graduated from college. But then there was something very private and secretive about Gene. He didn't have many close friends—only acquaintances. I was as close to him as anyone at the time and I still had no idea what put wind in his sails."

But it was still Fred whose professional dancing aspirations occupied Harriet. Paying for his lessons was a large pill for a thrifty woman to swallow, even though James was at that time doing well at Columbia. Her inquisitive eye alighted on the man who ran the dancing school, Lou Bolton, and she discovered to her joy that he was a hopeless businessman. She volunteered to run the school in return for free lessons for Fred and

was so successful that when, in 1929, the Wall Street Crash put James out of a job—a terrible blow after an unblemished service record—she managed to persuade Bolton to put up the capital for her to open her own school in Johnstown, Pennsylvania, about sixty-five miles from Pittsburgh, where her favorite brother, Gus, lived. Bolton found the weekly trek across the Allegheny mountains a nuisance, particularly in winter, and just as the Johnstown offshoot weekend school in the American Legion Hall began to pay off, he started to miss sessions. Whenever this happened Gene deputized, and the children loved him. Within a few months Gene learned how to be a fine teacher, a skill he continued to use throughout his choreographic life. Finding students was a struggle—but Gene's competitive instincts were once more to the fore as he and Harriet fought the only other dance school in town for the business. "Unlike the shmuck down the road who gave his pupils a little heel-and-toe, and after one lesson convinced their parents their little geniuses were dancing, we taught them properly," Gene said later. "We taught our kids to dance like professionals. We got them working at the barre, and though it could take a month before they mastered a step, it remained with them for the rest of their lives." During these tough times the lessons were often paid for in

RIGHT *By the age of eighteen Gene was already an accomplished teacher of dance, and Harriet's dreams of a legal career would soon be history.* ☆

services (one mother scrubbed the studio floor) or in kind, with Harriet frequently lugging sacks of vegetables back to Pittsburgh in the Kellys' ancient car. By 1931 Lou had opted out, Harriet was the sole owner of the dance studio, and all the Kelly kids were duly pressed into service.

Sometimes Gene and Kay would play the local country clubs: "We would do the obligatory ballroom bit," he later recalled, "and then a kind of jazz ballet item which, now I think about it, was pretty awful. But we did with aplomb and we got by. Naturally people were concerned to know if we were brother and sister—we told them: certainly not, we were a professional dance act touring the country. I'm not sure if we fooled them or not, but we did make $150 some nights— apart from talent we had chutzpah, which was crucial."

3. The Gene Kelly School of the Dance

Times were now tough at Kensington Street. James hadn't worked for two years and was drinking heavily, Gene's eldest brother Jim was also out of work, there was a Depression with no "green shoots" in sight, and the savings were dwindling fast. The family eked out a living from the money Fred could win by dancing at amateur nights, the fees paid by the students in Johnstown, and whatever odd jobs the other kids could find. Gene had won a place at Penn State University and somehow managed to keep up his grades— he was, after all, going to be a lawyer—work on

> "Like a boxer, I felt I had to keep honing my body finer and finer"
> **GENE KELLY**

a building site, jerk sodas three nights a week at the most expensive ice-cream parlour in town and still make a reputation as the college's best entertainer. He had a job pumping gas at the local petrol station and another rolling tires at the Firestone Tire and Rubber Company. With all these combined, he was able to pay his way in college and contribute a bit to the family budget.

RIGHT *In the summer of his first year in college, Gene took a job as a camp counselor. At Camp Porter, Pennsylvania, he put on weekly shows and developed his athletic style of dancing.* ☆

Despite this punishing schedule Gene was still trying to improve his dancing skills because his increasing reputation meant he had to keep expanding his repertoire of steps. He heard of a teacher who offered sixteen bars of different steps for ten dollars, but he learned what she had to teach in only two lessons and this was an expensive way to pick up steps when a ticket to any performer passing through Pittsburgh could be bought for fifty cents or less. Gene and Fred developed their own system of dance notation and, with Gene writing down the first sixteen bars of a visiting dancer and Fred the second, they managed to "steal" dozens of new steps for their own use.

In college and out, Gene was always on the lookout for new steps. At the theater he saw George M. Cohan and the jauntiness of his style impressed him. So did the innovative step-making of one of the great black tap-dancers, "Dancin'" Dotson, from whom he copied a number of early routines. He met a drummer-cum-tap-dancer, Jim Barry, with whom he teamed up for college functions. All big bands of the time had tap dancers setting the rhythms and Barry had traveled with a big band before going to Penn State. He encouraged Gene to make up his own steps to the rhythms he would set, and thus the choreographer was born. Another influence

was Frank Harrington, a New York trained black tap-dancer he much admired who was a teacher at Lou Bolton's studio, an experienced dancer who took a real interest in Gene's development.

Gene and Fred (or, more probably, Harriet) decided that forming themselves into a duo and playing nights all over the area would net Gene enough to pay his college costs and still leave the days free for studying. This set in train a period of performance experience of inestimable value to him. The act was composed of a few gags (lifted from such comics as Milton Berle), and a couple of song-and-dance numbers, and occasionally Fred would extend the act with a little magic. "Fred was like an accordionist," Gene said. "Never knew when to get off."

He himself hated playing the small clubs ("cloops" he and Fred called them in a contraction of "clubs" and "chicken coops"), which would pay them from five to twelve dollars for anything up to four shows a night. He learned to cope with indifferent pianists, drunken audiences and crooked employers who refused to pay, and with his own short fuse. Cope with, but not conquer. To the end of his life Gene had a real distaste for the small time. This stemmed, at least in part, from their treatment at the hands of the many small impresarios who took advantage of them. On one occasion an agent sent them to do two shows for five dollars; in the event they only got four and when Gene asked his agent to intervene, the agent merely demanded his fifty-cent commission. Gene then hit the agent so hard that he broke his own finger and had to spend what little money he'd made getting it fixed in the local hospital.

Gene found it difficult to control his urge to hit people who annoyed him.

"The audience threw coins on the stage, which embarrassed me terribly.... The first time it happened I looked at the guy who threw the coins, and was ready to punch him on the jaw—then other people started throwing money and as I couldn't go around punching them all I just had to grin and bear it. Fred, of course, took it all in his stride. He picked up the money, flashed a smile, and just went on dancing. But I was mortified, shocked and ashamed. I realize now it was all good experience, though at the time I was just ready to die of humiliation."

Fred enjoyed the rough and tumble of one-night stands and outwitting the customers, while Gene dreamed of attentive, respectful audiences and big-budget show dancing.

He began to pursue those dreams at the end of his first year in college, when he was hired as a camp counselor at a YMCA summer camp with a special responsibility to put on weekly shows. This had a number of advantages. The $150 he earned was enough to pay his college tuition for the next year; he gained valuable experience as an organizer and choreographer, and, because the talent he had to work with was largely that of young athletes, he was able to demonstrate to their and to his satisfaction the physical parallels between sports and dance, an observation which was subsequently to form the basis of his dancing style.

This experience also gave him the confidence to accept when the local synagogue asked him to take over from Lou Bolton the staging of its annual fundraising show. Beth Shalom wanted a full-length show and Gene didn't hesitate to say he could do it. His first show was a triumph. At the age of nineteen he had directed, choreographed, and, with Fred, starred in *Revue of Revues*, a show for which he trained all the synagogue children by teaching them basketball or football as well as dance, thereby reassuring the boys that dancing wasn't sissy. "He worked so fantastically well with the children," said one Beth Shalom Sisterhood member, "that practically every child in the Squirrel Hill neighborhood wanted to attend his classes. You could tell he was a star. He had this incredible magnetism, and he could get children to do anything he wanted." Another fifteen dollars a week went into the Kelly family kitty, a salary he earned from the synagogue Sisterhood for seven years until he left for Broadway.

All these ongoing friendships and contacts —with Jews, with blacks, with Christians of other denominations—gave Gene a lifelong contempt for racial bigotry. In college the humiliation of realizing that, as a Catholic, he could not join the same fraternities as his Protestant or Jewish friends made him angry enough to try to break the system. He and two others, a Protestant called Johnnie Napoleon and Eddie Malamud, who was Jewish, formed themselves into a triumvirate to fight both the discrimination and the appalling initiation practices of fraternities in general. They failed but, as Gene said later: "The prejudice I encountered at college made a terrific impression on me ... It had a lot to do with my thinking and future outlook on life."

Beth Shalom also gave him a room to give private lessons in, but The Gene Kelly Studio of the Dance soon outgrew its basement and moved into the ballroom of the Pittsburgh Hotel. Life was pretty full: college during the weekdays, gigs with Fred in the evenings, teaching in Johnstown on Saturdays from 8 a.m. until 10 p.m., back to Pittsburgh to mass on Sunday mornings followed by Beth Shalom on Sunday afternoons. He picked up a few

high-paying engagements. One he remembers particularly was a high-tone country club which he took on with Jay, by now a teacher with a Master's degree but still helping out with the family business. They earned $150 for one evening, more than he'd ever earned with Fred, for two numbers.

He worked out in a gym whenever he could, learned French and Italian, visited speakeasies with his friend "Doc" Steinberg, and, whenever he got a break, went and performed, alone or with one of his sisters or Fred, anywhere a booking could be found. The family was managing slightly better financially but still, every penny helped. During the 1932 Chicago World's Fair he and Fred worked from six to ten shows a day, under different names, and even stood in for each other if one found a better gig.

In 1932 Gene decided to expand the school in Johnstown and to take over the artistic management from Harriet. It was now called The Gene Kelly School of the Dance and, after a rocky start, it did well. He was just twenty but he was now responsible for a successful business. Predictably, Harriet kept him and Fred and Louise on allowances, while Jim and Jay were expected to earn their own livings and were therefore no longer part of the Kelly budget. The school flourished, mostly because for the next five years Gene staged an annual summer revue with all his students. The local newspapers waxed enthusiastic and his first reviews were ecstatic: "Mr Kelly's work with children speaks for itself. He has presented clearly and thoughtfully every type of dancing in a manner that cannot be surpassed ... the only kiddies' show to hold an engagement a full week on any legitimate stage in the United States." These shows—*Johnstown on Parade*; *Gene Kelly's Kiddies' Vodvil*; *The Talk of the Town Revue*—used all his students (by 1933 there were 150 of them in Johnstown alone) plus a full orchestra.

James Kelly, out of work since 1929, now joined the family business to run the accounting side of the schools. With two thriving schools and the performing side of things, poor Harriet was at her wit's end. Fortunately, James loved it and Harriet was then free to accompany her sons to nearly all their engagements. The success of the school in Johnstown now meant a constant stream of talented young dancers for Gene to incorporate into the increasingly elaborate shows he was mounting. Eventually he put together a small orchestra from high-school musicians and had a full production variety show that he charged out to local towns at seventy-five dollars. "As we did more and more shows, my father found himself with a full-time job on his hands for which I think

LEFT *After graduating in 1933, Gene entered law school, but after a few weeks he was back at the family dancing school and the die was cast.* ☆

he was very grateful, particularly as he had given up drinking and needed something to take its place."

Gene graduated with a degree in economics in 1933 and celebrated by starting to learn ballet. He reasoned that "real" dance training required a classical background and he couldn't teach what he didn't know. He worked so hard at perfecting his technique that when the Ballets Russes de Monte Carlo came through town he auditioned and, even though he had started so late, was offered a place in the company. But, after discussion with Harriet, he turned it down, practical as ever. "As much as I loved classical ballet, I had to face the fact that my style of dancing was more modern. I really couldn't see myself doing *Swan Lake* and *The Sleeping Beauty* for the next twenty years, living off two dollars a week and a doughnut."

It was time for law school, the fulfillment of all Harriet's dreams for him. The trouble was, he hated it. Never having questioned what his mother had presented as his Manifest Destiny, when it came to it he was bored and restless. He lasted only a few weeks before selling his lawbooks and heading back gratefully to his students. His school was becoming a Mecca for touring dancers and he was soon discovered by the big Pittsburgh professional theaters which now saw no reason

to bring in a New York director or choreographer when they had Gene Kelly living in their midst. He earned $150 a show from the Pittsburgh Playhouse, while the university paid him a princely $350 for each of the *Cap and Gown* shows he directed, choreographed and starred in. One of those who sought him out was the New York choreographer Robert Alton, and they became friends.

He learned, and taught in the schools, all the latest dances being popularized by the movies, such as the Carioca and the Continental. Astaire and Rogers were the King and Queen of screen dance and, although Gene himself disliked ballroom dancing, it earned quick money and made him study Astaire's movies carefully. He made those dances work for him, as he would do with every other movement discipline throughout his performing life. He was ready for the big time.

By 1937 almost every aspect of Gene's life was going well. The schools were making money and the family had stabilized: Jim was now a successful commercial artist and Jay was a respected teacher, James was an integral member of the family firm and Gene was a popular teacher, performer and choreographer, getting plenty of work and enjoying the company of fellow dancers from all over the country. But Gene was ambitious and, although he was now a biggish fish, Pittsburgh was a small pond. Fred and Louise were now old enough to take over Gene's role in the schools, and the senior Kellys were still in charge. So when he received an offer to choreograph one number in a Broadway revue Gene thought that he was ready and set off for New York.

Unfortunately, he wasn't yet used to the ways of Broadway and was disgusted to discover that between the offer and his arrival in New York the plans had changed and he was now merely to appear in the number rather than choreograph it. Four days later he was back in Pittsburgh.

In April 1938 Gene got his first extended job as a choreographer when the Pittsburgh Playhouse invited him to work on a musical revue, *Hold your Hats*, written entirely by Charles Gaynor; the show ran for a month, with Gene appearing in six of the sketches and doing one solo ("La Cumparsita") which would, eight years later, be the basis for his elaborate Spanish number in MGM's *Anchors Aweigh*. It was partly his huge success in this revue that encouraged him to take another crack at the Big Apple. This time he was determined—as only Harriet Kelly's son could have been—that he was going to succeed.

On August 5th, 1938, Harriet took him to Pittsburgh Station, where he bought a one-way ticket to New York. He took with him a small suitcase and $200. Gene Kelly was going to be a star.

4. You Gotta Have Hart: The "Pal Joey" Story

His second brush with Broadway hard-noses came when he auditioned for *Sing Out The News*, a new musical by Harold Rome. While he was watching the other hopefuls, he came to the conclusion that none could hold a candle to him, so when he was offered a featured role in the show he tried to negotiate a higher salary than the producers suggested. Perhaps not surprisingly, they balked. Gene later explained his action to Clive Hirschhorn with typical pugnacity. "I wasn't going to accept the same salary a chorus girl was getting for wriggling her arse when I was doing a helluva lot more in the show. They wanted to exploit me, but I wasn't going to have it. I had to begin this game as I intended finishing it, so I walked out of the theater without a job."

> *"If Joey must be acted, Mr Kelly can do it"*
>
> BROOKS ATKINSON

RIGHT *A fur-clad Mary Martin sings her "Siberia" number in Cole Porter's* Leave it to Me. *The Eskimo on her right, in his first Broadway show, is Gene Kelly, of whom she later said: "I've never known anybody who worked so hard perfecting his art."* ☆

Clearly Gene needed some professional guidance, and he got it from his friend Robert Alton, who introduced him to his own agent, Johnny Darrow. He immediately arranged an audition for him with the Shuberts, who liked what they saw. Darrow over-played his hand by trying to get them to pay this unknown dancer $300 a week (in 1938) after they had generously offered him $150. They promptly withdrew the offer. Instead of being furious with his new agent, Gene was magnanimous, probably because of his own over-reaching in the same area. When Alton heard about Darrow's miscalculation he felt somewhat responsible and immediately offered Gene a small feature role in a new show, *Leave it to Me*, which he accepted gratefully at half what the Shuberts had offered him.

Now that he had work he moved into his first home, a flat he shared with another dancer, and started his first serious love affair. The girl was Helene Marlowe, a dancer he had met the previous year at the Pittsburgh Playhouse. She was more interested than he was in the modern dance explosion of the 1930s that included the work of Martha Graham, Doris Humphreys and Charles Weidman, and it was with her that Gene began to work out what kind of dancing he wanted to do. Fascinated as he was by their new shapes and rhythms, and even the strange new sounds

being developed to accompany them, he himself, a traditional boy from Pittsburgh, dreamed about dancing to the music of Cole Porter and Jerome Kern. With his first Broadway show, he got his chance.

Cole Porter's *Leave it to Me* opened on Broadway at the Imperial Theater on November 21st, 1938. As the war in Europe appeared to have been averted by Neville Chamberlain's "Peace in our Time", it was a suitably political satire about a deeply confused American ambassador being sent to Russia because nobody in Washington could bear the sight of him. The official stars of the show were Victor Moore, Sophie Tucker and Tamara but on the first night it was stolen from all of them by a young girl from Texas called Mary Martin. She, with her one number, "My Heart Belongs to Daddy," full of sexual double meanings, made the most starry overnight debut in the history of Broadway to date.

As she was later to recall: "I played a dumb cluck who had urgently to be shipped out of town, all the way to Siberia. I arrived there dressed to the teeth, with even a fur hat. There were six boys, dancers, who had to meet me wearing Eskimo suits and we did a dance number in which there were a lot of lifts, so the boys would pick me up, sling me around, and pass me from hand to hand. One of those Eskimos was Gene Kelly; he was just a kid then on his first Broadway job, but I liked him from the very first day. He was so talented, had so much drive. I've never known anybody who worked so hard perfecting his art. Of all the boys, he was the one who came into the theater every day of his life to work for hours and hours and hours on the stage. From the beginning, I knew he was going to be somebody very great. I couldn't anticipate then that he was going to change the whole look and spirit of Hollywood musical films— but I knew his drive and determination were boundless, and all through his career he danced with the verve of that young man I first knew."

There were a few people in New York, apart from Mary Martin and Robert Alton, who already recognized Kelly's unique talent. Gene's agent, Johnny Darrow, knew that John Murray Anderson was working on a new Little Theater revue, which was due to open three months after *Leave it to Me*. He offered Gene the lead in *One for the Money*, but the producers of *Leave it to Me* told Gene that if he left their show he would never work for them again. After careful thought, and considering that the new show was offering $115 a week, roughly twice what he had been earning, Gene decided to take the risk and go for it. In the show, he was required to sing and dance in eight routines. It also gave him his

first crack at dialog. "You never get paid much for just dancing. In that second show somebody gave me a line to say and I realized they'd have to pay me more to speak. And I thought, hey, this is easy."

It was a formative experience in other ways, too, as Gene recalled: "I learned more about staging a show from the director, John Murray Anderson, than from anybody else in the business. During rehearsals I never took my eyes off him. His timing was superb and he could create any mood he wanted through his brilliant use of lighting. He'd watch a song, then make one simple suggestion that would turn a good number into a hit. Where other directors of that period, like Minnelli and George Abbott, knew how to construct a scene, you could always see the seams ... with Murray all you saw was the magic and wonderment of the effect ... I would say no one has had as great an influence on my work as Anderson, and when I went into pictures I tried to adopt his approach to color by insisting, for many of my numbers, on certain tints and washes."

After its Broadway run *One for the Money* went out on the road and because Anderson was otherwise engaged Gene was allowed to restage it with a replacement cast. After the tour he spent the summer of 1939 as resident choreographer at the summer stock company in Westport, Connecticut. "I learned to be an actor by working in summer stock. I learned to do it all, some of it maybe not so well, but I learned a lot that year." His most exciting assignment at Westport was to work with the legendary Paul Robeson on a musical of Eugene O'Neill's *The Emperor Jones*, which never made it to Broadway but allowed Kelly to devise a series of highly charged dances for an all-black company from Harlem. One more good thing came out of this first summer at Westport. The stage manager spent his winter months working for the prestigious Theater Guild, the premier production company for Broadway plays, and he knew that its first offering for the upcoming season was William Saroyan's *The Time of Your Life*. An actor playing Harry, the ever-hopeful hoofer, had been fired on the road and Kelly was called in to play a role that might have been tailored for him, that of a gentle dancer who is one of the group of losers in that San Francisco waterfront saloon. The best of the reviews went to Eddie Dowling and Julie Haydon but the *New York Times* added: "Some memorable scenes by Gene Kelly and William Bendix."

The play ran throughout the Broadway season of 1939–40, won a Pulitzer Prize, and was the first to establish Kelly as a dance-actor rather than just a hoofer. When it closed Gene, immensely richer in experience and professional standing, returned to Westport

for his second season there. While there, he choreographed the first musical version of Lynn Riggs's *Green Grow the Lilacs*. Four years and several incarnations later, this was to open on Broadway (with the ballet choreographer Agnes de Mille instead of Kelly's dances) as *Oklahoma!* Gene's last show that season required him to be master of ceremonies for an intimate revue starring Betty Comden and Adolph Green. As The Revuers, these two remarkable talents had originated at a New York nightclub, the Village Vanguard, where their particular brand of humor had been augmented by their friend, Judy Holliday. By the time they reached Westport, Judy was on her way to becoming a big star and, while they were still performing as a double act (indeed, at the time of writing they still are), they were metamorphosing into the lyricists and bookwriters who were to give Gene not only the movie version of their 1938 Broadway hit *On the Town*, and the later *Take Me Out to the Ballgame*, but also the book for *Singin' in the Rain*. Although Gene had no way of knowing it at the time, he later said: "We loved each other from the start and I can say that a lot of my career rests on their shoulders."

The show they worked on with Gene was called *The Magazine Page* and, as Betty Comden said: "Gene came into the show at the last minute and I remember thinking how attractive and how full of vitality he was." The morning after the opening, the reviewer for the local *Bridgeport Post* agreed: "The dancing of Gene Kelly, an added starter not listed on the programme, especially his demonstration of the various types of tap-dancers, was the evening's high spot."

Gene made a deep impression on Adolph Green too: "To me, he was then just an energetic young man who looked much younger than his twenty-seven years. He was a hoofer with something extra hidden away. He had this terrific outgoing quality combined with a street-boy earthiness which was extremely appealing. You just knew he was going places and, when I saw his act in Westport, I was knocked out immediately .... Everything that he was later to become was already there in a nugget. His qualities were immediately apparent, and the surprising thing was, when you first looked at him, what struck you most was his charm and his clean-cut good looks. You didn't think of him as a dancer at all. But the minute he took off, it was a different story. He was full of grace and vitality, and what I remember most was the effect he had on an audience. They just loved him. He could do no wrong. There was this magic—this "star quality" he exuded. His dancing was very athletic and he had the

wonderful ability to make the most complicated things look ridiculously simple."

Gene returned to New York without much money and moved into a fleapit apartment with a friend called Dick Dwenger, who was so hard up that in lieu of rent he would play the piano for Gene to practice. Bob Alton suggested that Gene should apply for the job of dance director for *Billy Rose's Diamond Horseshoe*. "Rose was the hardest, toughest man I have ever met in this business," Kelly recalled, "but I'm still grateful to him, because he was the man who gave me my first real job as a Broadway choreographer." Rose had wanted Alton, who was unavailable, but both he and John Murray Anderson recommended Gene. On the telephone Rose gave Gene an outline of the show and demanded to know whether he was capable of doing it. Gene paused for the briefest of moments and then, without any further opportunity to think, poured out his preliminary ideas in what Rose called a "mental audition." Gene said later: "At the audition he was mean and rude and negative, so I swore at him in return. He told me never to talk to him that way and I replied that I would never want to work for him anyway. This amused him enough that he invited me to come to his office and tell him my ideas for the show. These he liked and he offered me $115 a week. I said I couldn't work for that so he added another twenty dollars. The following day I went to work."

But the best thing of all about *Billy Rose's Diamond Horseshoe*, at any rate for Gene, was that he also transferred a sixteen-year-old dancer from his International Casino Supper Club. Her name was Betsy Blair and she came to audition on the wrong day, asking an attractive young man for directions. He asked her whether she was a good dancer and, when she said she was, Gene said he would see her the following day. The producers wanted to eliminate her as too skinny and flat-chested, but Kelly rescued her by assuring the others that she "was a *very* good dancer," and she was hired. She worked harder than anyone except Gene and rapidly fell desperately in love with him. Although she occasionally had lunch with him and Dick Dwenger, now the *Diamond Horseshoe* rehearsal pianist, he was still living with Helene Marlowe and displayed no particular interest in Betsy. But slowly he began to notice her. Like him she was an ordinary person from an ordinary family (mother a teacher, father an insurance clerk) and he felt comfortable with her. They were married a year later and had their only child, Kerry, a year after that.

Unbeknownst to Gene, his next job, the one that would make him a star overnight, was already lined up. The composer Richard Rodgers had been to see *The Time of Your Life* one night earlier that year. "In the small role of an aspiring entertainer I saw an especially engaging young man named Gene Kelly. The stage was aglow with life whenever he appeared and his dancing was superb. The next day I wrote to John O'Hara that I had found his Pal Joey."

What Rodgers and his already-ailing lyricist Lorenz Hart had in mind was not a musical based on any one plot, but something that would borrow scenes and characters from the brilliantly acerbic stories about Joey that O'Hara had now been publishing for some years in the *New Yorker* magazine. "As I expected," Rodgers remembered, "Larry Hart was equally enthusiastic about the project. He had spent thousands of hours in exactly the

LEFT *Gene's performance as the amoral Joey Evans made him an immediate star.* ☆

kind of seedy Broadway atmosphere depicted in these stories and was thoroughly familiar with the Pal Joeys of this world. Not only would the show be totally different from anything we had ever done before, it would be different from anything else that anyone had ever tried. This alone was reason enough to make us want to do it."

Pal Joey required a leading man with the unusual ability not only to sing and dance but also to act well enough to create an ingratiating, unscrupulous nightclub entertainer called Joey Evans who races through his life using people, predominantly women, never aware of the pain that he has brought them.

George Abbott was to be the director. "I remember a terrifying audition for Rodgers and O'Hara and Abbott," said Gene: "...the only one of the team who was absent was the only one I already knew. I had gotten to know Larry Hart in local saloons, not Sardi's or the Stork Club, but the cheap bars around Eighth Avenue and 45th where Larry could usually be found. He loved actors and dancers and he loved to hang around with them so I got to know him, not closely but in a fun kind of way. He'd come in and we'd be around the bar and he'd tell us stories, chomping on his cigar. Hart was a marvelous little fellow and, of course, we all admired him for his great talent

and so he always had a ready audience. We all looked up to him."

All the same, Kelly nearly lost the job by making what could have been a terrible mistake at the audition. "I did a really stupid thing, in using a Rodgers and Hart song, 'I Didn't Know What Time It Was.' I was naive enough not even to think about this; I just thought I'd do a ballad for them, an 'up' song. I didn't even know it was a Rodgers and Hart ballad. Years later, when I became a director and producer myself, I learned how songwriters hate this kind of thing because it looks like you're currying favor." After the audition was over O'Hara, who hadn't said a word throughout, called from the back of the stalls: "That's it. Take him." It took another three weeks for them all to decide but eventually Gene had secured the job of a lifetime. Darrow drew up a contract for $350 a week, far from a princely sum for a starring role but, as he explained: "As far as I was concerned, he could have played Pal Joey for nothing: it was that important a show."

Pal Joey was an historic landmark in the development of Broadway musicals. It freed them from their usual soft-focus romantic structure and gave a harder edge to characters and situations than had previously been seen. It proved, for the very first time, a decade before *Guys and Dolls*, that the genre could cope with a brainy, cynical, seedy under-class as well as the bland upper-class, white-tie-and-tails brainlessness of most of what had gone before. That orginal cast in 1940, led by Kelly and Vivienne Segal (later also to star in *Guys and Dolls*), was an amazing collection of unknowns on their way to some kind of stardom. June Havoc, sister of the stripper Gypsy Rose Lee (later to be immortalized in Sondheim and Styne's *Gypsy*) played here the wonderfully named Gladys Bumps. Two other members of that cast, Robert Mulligan and a sixteen-year-old Stanley Donen, became triumphant film directors, and Van Johnson was there too.

They opened on Christmas night 1940, at the Ethel Barrymore Theater, where it was to stay for 374 performances. The initial reviews were surprisingly mixed, for the show if not for Gene. The *New Yorker*, the original source of the material on which it was based, got right behind it at once but *Time Magazine* took the opportunity to comment on "Cigar-chewing Hart, the pint-sized genius with the two-quart capacity." The feeling about the score was generally ecstatic, which was hardly surprising, given that it included "Betwitched, Bothered and Bewildered," "Zip," "You Mustn't Kick It Around,"and "I Could Write A Book," all written by Rodgers and Hart in a three-week blaze of activity. This was to be

Kelly's only starring role in a Broadway musical. At the cast party given by Larry Hart they all read the most important critic of the day, Brooks Atkinson of the *New York Times* who, taking the high moral ground, wrote: "How can you ever get sweet water from a foul well?" Hearing that, Larry burst into tears and locked himself in his bedroom for a couple of days with several bottles of scotch.

But even Atkinson, having written "Pal Joey offers everything but a good time," was forced to acknowledge Gene Kelly as a new star: "Mr O'Hara has drawn a pitiless portrait of this small-time braggart and the company he keeps; and Gene Kelly, who distinguished himself as the melancholy hoofer in *The Time of Your Life*, plays Joey with remarkable accuracy. His cheap and flamboyant unction, his nervous cunning and his trickiness are qualities that Kelly catches without forgetting the fright or the gaudiness ... Kelly is also a brilliant tap-dancer ("makes with the feet" as it goes in his vernacular) and his performance on both scores is triumphant. If Joey must be acted, Mr Kelly can do it."

But this turned out to be one of those shows for which long queues began to form around the box office and, at the first revival, twelve years later, Atkinson totally reversed his original notice. Gene himself was under no illusions about his good fortune: "It was just a

RIGHT *In Pal Joey Gene was able to use his style of dancing both to create a character and to manipulate the audience.* ☆

case of being the right man in the right place at the right time and having the tremendous luck to play a part like that. With a script by John O'Hara, songs by Rodgers and Hart, and a director like Abbott. I think I did well in it because it gave me a chance to use my own style of dancing to create a character. I wanted to dance to American music and at that time nobody else was doing it. And Joey was a meaty character to play. He was completely amoral. After some scenes I could feel the waves of hate coming from the audience. Then I'd smile at them and dance and it would relax them. It was interesting to be able to use the character to manipulate the audience."

It was another Broadway critic, John Martin, who at this time came up with far and away the most perceptive account of Gene's talent: "If Kelly were to be judged exclusively by his actual performance of the dance routines that fall to him, he would still be a good dancer, but when his dancing is seen in the fuller light of *Pal Joey* he becomes an exceptional one. A tap-dancer who can characterize his routines and turn them into an integral element of an imaginative theatrical whole would seem to me pretty close to unique. He is not only glib-footed, he has a feeling for comment and content that both gives his dancing personal distinction and raises it several notches as a theater art."

5. Love from Judy

But Kelly was not to spend any more of his time on Broadway. During the run of *Pal Joey* he began to receive a number of offers from the film studios—notably from MGM which is, of course, where he finally ended up. An MGM writer had alerted one of its producers, Arthur Freed, to Gene's performance and he in turn had persuaded Louis B. Mayer, the MGM mogul, to go along to the Ethel Barrymore Theater to see for himself. The following day, through Johnny Darrow, he invited Gene to his New York office and announced that his *Pal Joey* performance was so strong that he wanted Gene to sign an MGM contract without even asking him to make a screen test. Gene was thrilled and the two men shook hands on the deal.

"I arrived in Hollywood twenty pounds overweight and as strong as an ox. But if I put on a white tie and tails like Astaire, I still looked like a truck driver"

GENE KELLY

RIGHT *In his first film for MGM, the 1942* For Me and My Gal, *Gene formed a mutually rewarding partnership with the twenty-year-old Judy Garland.* ☆

Several days later an MGM minion contacted Gene to arrange, he explained, for a screen test. A mistake, Gene told him; go check with Mr Mayer. Whereupon a memo from Louis B. was produced, in which Mayer insisted on a test. Gene was incensed: a deal was a deal. He wrote Mayer a furious letter telling him in no uncertain terms that he was no longer interested in working for him. Mayer, he said, was a right-wing establishment punk who had lied to him. On principle Gene was not prepared to throw away his entire future in the movies. His childhood friend Jules Steinberg wasn't surprised. "There was something very unworldly about Gene. White was white and black was black. If he had an idea in his head about something, he wasn't going to let anything come between it and him."

But then the future arrived in the shape of David O. Selznick. Although he was Louis B. Mayer's son-in-law, Gene liked him immediately. He offered Gene a seven-year contract with his own independent studio, at a starting salary of $750 a week, to go west and this time the "no-screen-test" agreement was honored. It was to begin three months hence, in October 1941, which would allow Gene time to finish the run of *Pal Joey* and also choreograph the Broadway musical *Best Foot Forward*, a fluffy little show directed by George Abbott which provided Gene with his first Broadway choreography credit. In fact, he did rather more than make the dances. Abbott was having trouble with the show and asked Gene to play "show doctor" which he did.

Best Foot Forward was to prove surprisingly durable, despite its fragile plot about a Hollywood starlet going to the annual prom at a fan's high school. The original Broadway run outlasted *Pal Joey* by some fifty or so performances. The movie, with its original stars, Nancy Walker and June Allyson, also gave Lucille Ball one of her great early opportunities, while a 1963 revival in turn introduced a seventeen-year-old Liza Minnelli to off-Broadway.

Having settled that company onto Broadway, Gene finally broke with Helene and decided he really was serious about Betsy, serious enough to want to marry her before he went to California. They were married in a Catholic ceremony in Philadelphia on September 24th with the entire Kelly clan and all Betsy's relations present in serried ranks. They set off across the country and their honeymoon was spent settling into their new home in California.

Once there, Gene took up his contract with David O. Selznick, only to find immediately that there were two major problems. Firstly, Selznick had never made a musical in his life and wasn't about to start now. Secondly,

RIGHT *A private performance for his wife Betsy and their daughter Kerry.* ☆

having just had a run of huge successes (*A Star is Born*, *The Prisoner of Zenda*, *Tom Sawyer*, *Rebecca*, and, above all, *Gone with the Wind*) he was in no mood to make another picture in the near future. As usual, however, he was prepared to loan out his stars for vast profits to anybody else who wanted them: thus it was that Gene was first of all miscast as the young priest in *The Keys of the Kingdom*. With some difficulty Gene talked Selznick, by now a regular visitor at the Kellys' Laurel Canyon house and one of his drinking buddies, out of the assignment and the role was eventually played by Gregory Peck. The single-minded Selznick then told Kelly that if he wouldn't play the lead he should at least play the role of the Scots doctor. Kelly pointed out that his Scots accent was non-existent but Selznick, never to be deterred, sent him for five weeks to a dialect coach. At the end of that time a screen test was made which David and Gene viewed together. The sound of their guffaws echoed down the corridors. Even David had to agree that Gene was terrible beyond all belief and Thomas Mitchell was duly hired to replace him. Despite their friendship Gene was convinced that Selznick, never a man to dwell on his mistakes, would soon realize that he had nothing for him and would ship him back to New York by the first train. Instead, David sold half of Gene's contract on to MGM.

It was there, working for the hated Louis B. Mayer, five months after his arrival in California that Arthur Freed offered Gene his first movie musical. With the luck of the Irish, Kelly fell on his feet. The movie was *For Me and My Gal*, his co-star was to be Judy Garland, and they loved each other from then on. As Gene recalled: "At that time, I was constantly being thrown by the piecemeal way in which pictures were being made. I knew nothing about playing to the camera and I didn't even know whether I was being shot close, medium or long, or about the intricate business of hitting all the marks laid out on the studio floor for the movements of the actors. It was Judy who pulled me through. She was very kind and helpful, more helpful than even she realized because I used to watch her to find out what I had to do. Judy was only twenty, but she had been in pictures for six years. I was amazed at her skill; she knew every mark and every move. All I could do for her then was to help with her dancing. She wasn't a dancer, but she could pick up a step instantly, and as a singer she was incredible— she only had to hear a melody once and it was locked in her mind. I learned a great deal about making movies doing this one, and much of it was due to Judy Garland."

It was in fact Judy who got him the job; this was the first time she achieved solo billing above the title but she had seen Gene dance on Broadway and was so impressed that she convinced Arthur Freed, head of the MGM musicals department, to cast him as her leading man. Originally this role had been promised to George Murphy but, under pressure from Freed and Garland, the director, the legendary Busby Berkeley, gave the part to Kelly. George Murphy grudgingly agreed to take the second lead as the faithful friend who never gets the girl, a role he was then condemned to play for most of the rest of his career. Berkeley was understandably irritated at being over-ruled by his producer and rode Gene very hard. Kelly had to keep his mind on the objective, which was a successful film debut, and tried to shrug off the bad feeling. In this, Judy Garland was his biggest ally. "Without her," he often said, gratefully, "my first few weeks at MGM would have been even more miserable than they were." But Gene was not, in fact, unhappy with his first outing, particularly his debut as a screen actor. "Some of the best acting I ever did was in *For Me and My Gal*, though I never thought of competing with Barrymore, or Tracy or Franchot Tone. There is a scene with Judy in that picture in which we just talked—and that's as good as anything I have ever done, because I played it easily and naturally. Nothing I did in most of my straight movies was ever as good, and although on Broadway I was a damned good actor (I could hit that fourth balcony with no trouble at all), I needed to see 3,000 pairs of eyes in order to do it. On the screen it was a different story altogether."

The story of *For Me and My Gal* doesn't bear too much analysis. It concerns a troupe of traveling players arriving in a small town and trying to balance their amorous entanglements with the desire to make it big on Broadway, and the various complications engendered by the First World War. For Gene, the problems of a first film were eased somewhat by the fact that he was again playing a charming but conceited young hoofer, a character not a million miles removed from Pal Joey himself— which is, of course, the main reason why Freed wanted Gene to play it.

When *For Me and My Gal* was given a sneak preview in Westwood, eighty-five percent of the audience said they thought that George Murphy, not Gene Kelly, ought to have won Judy Garland in the end. So Louis B. Mayer ordered the recall of the entire cast in order for new scenes, incorporating footage from Vidor's *The Big Parade*, to be added so that Kelly's character could redeem himself by becoming a war hero. This necessitated three weeks of additional production, but the new version satisfied everyone—except, of course, George Murphy.

The film was sentimental and forgettable but there were eighteen musical numbers, including the three that Gene and Judy sing together: the title song, the great jazz-dance "Ballin' The Jack" and the schmaltzy "When You Wore a Tulip." Kelly also had his solo "tramp dance" and though the reviews were far from ecstatic, several did refer to Kelly as a likable new find.

During the long five months that Gene and Betsy had been living like movie-stars, (thanks to regular checks from David Selznick), but not actually making a movie, their little house had become a Mecca for the younger film colony denizens, including Selznick himself. They loved to play charades, and so serious was Gene about playing what came to be known as The Game that teams were recruited from all over Hollywood. Nearly every night there would be a full house at the Kellys' home with every guest involved in the action, which was played against the clock. Gladys Cooper's daughter, Sally, who was only nine at the time, was, she recalls, rather good at The Game and Gene was anxious for her to be on his team. "Gene didn't like to lose. The trouble was that I got so good that all the grown-ups resented being beaten by a child and I was usually sent home to bed just as things were getting really interesting." Both Gene and Betsy were incredibly fast at guessing the phrases set by an independent score-keeper and acted out by the opposing teams, and everybody who was in Hollywood at the time, from Betty Comden to Marti Stevens, has described the extreme competitiveness and physicality of The Game and its principal participants. These evenings continued until the movie colony began to disintegrate in the 1970s; when Gene and Betsy moved from their rented house into a more permanent residence to accommodate the baby whom Betsy was by now expecting, their neighbors were delighted to be rid of the noise habitually made by the Kellys' guests.

Meanwhile, Selznick, still part owner of Gene, kept telling him he was wasting his time in musicals but totally failed to come up with any alternative. Even at MGM, where the Arthur Freed unit was in full production, they couldn't think what to do with him to follow up *For Me and My Gal*. None of their other current musicals seemed to have a role suitable for him so, for his second film, Gene was thrust into a wartime B-movie. Originally called *Skyway to Glory* but later given the even less appealing title of *Pilot Number 5*, this was a routine programmer with Kelly rather curiously cast as a moody Italian-American pilot who narrates a tale of courage and corruption in Java as it is attacked by the Japanese. As Gene later noted: "The picture started out to be much bigger and stronger than it finally emerged. The original idea was a statement against fascism, to draw a parallel between the malpractice of political power in America and the kind of fascism overseas that had drawn America into the war. We intended a warning against fascism at home, based on the memory of Huey Long and the danger of one man gaining control of a state. But MGM lost its nerve about taking any kind of political stand at that time, which is not hard to understand: we were in the entertainment business and this was wartime. So the script was totally de-fanged." Gene, always his own sternest critic, later told Clive Hirschhorn: "I was trying to give a performance all the time and that's about the worst thing you can do. In *Pilot Number 5*, I looked fine in the long shots but the close-ups weren't any good. In fact, I've never learned how to do a close-up the way, say, Spencer Tracy did. Orson Welles once said that the camera close-up was kind to a chosen few. Tracy was one of the few. I wasn't. I had a tendency to overact." Reviews for Gene were at best condescending ("the dancer can act"), so it was with considerable relief that he got back to a musical.

In fact, Gene would have taken whatever MGM threw at him; he and Betsy were now the proud parents of a daughter, Kerry, and a regular studio cheque was an essential part of

RIGHT *A 1943 studio photograph of MGM's rising star, already with four films to his name.* ☆

life in the Hollywood Hills. Their close circle of Game-playing friends now included an eager funny youngster with an attractive voice, a nice personality and large, brown, glamorous eyes, like those of a gazelle. Although he was known around the place as "the kid," his name was Stanley Donen. Another frequent visitor was an ex-chorus dancer called Jeanne Coyne whom Gene had first taught when she was seven years old at his Pittsburgh dancing academy, and who had later understudied Betsy in a couple of Broadway shows.

The new MGM musical was what many considered to be yet another Hollywood travesty of a Broadway classic. This one was Cole Porter's *Dubarry Was a Lady*, which had opened in triumph on Broadway in December, 1939 with Ethel Merman and Bert Lahr. Neither was reckoned big enough with the cinema-going public to risk using again and they were therefore replaced for the film with Lucille Ball and Red Skelton, with Gene demoted to third billing as, yet again, a song-and-dance man. But the real problem here was that out of Porter's original twenty-song score only three numbers survived, the rest being the work of no fewer than six other songwriters. Luckily for Gene, he had two of the Porter originals, "Do I Love You, Do I?" and the chorus number "Friendship," so he was able to escape with reasonable reviews, (as was Zero Mostel, making his film debut). Otherwise critics were eager to report that Skelton and Ball were no match for the original stage stars.

In an active but far from satisfactory 1943 Gene was to make two more films, neither of which could be said to have advanced his career in any real way. The first of these was a genuine curiosity: *Thousands Cheer* (not to be confused with the Irving Berlin wartime stage show *As Thousands Cheer*) featured an all-star line-up of the twenty biggest names on MGM's payroll. These included Mickey Rooney, doing for the third time on film his impersonations of Clark Gable and Lionel Barrymore; Red Skelton, in a sketch with the child star Margaret O'Brien about who could eat the most ice cream; Frank Morgan, the Wizard of Oz himself, playing a phony doctor examining Lucille Ball rather too closely; Eleanor Powell, doing her celebrated tap-dance; Lena Horne with a definitive "Honeysuckle Rose;" June Allyson, Gloria de Haven, and Virginia O'Brien singing "A Little Spanish Town;" and an uneasy coupling of Judy Garland and José Iturbi, the Spanish pianist and conductor who would now be a regular MGM artist, in a raucous jazz number. Others, equally random, included Ann Sothern and Mary Astor. "We've got more stars

than there are in the heavens," Louis B. Mayer once famously remarked, "all of them except for that damned Mouse over at Disney."

Thousands Cheer was one of those wartime morale-boosters. Gene played a circus star drafted against his will, who falls in love with Kathryn Grayson, as the daughter of his camp commander. She puts on a camp show, and invites various famous entertainers to perform for the troops who are just about to depart for the war in Europe. There were many such shows at this time, but probably none boasted the feast of talent in Grayson's celluloid version. The plot wasn't up to much, which wasn't a problem, given the song and dance numbers from the amazing array of guest stars.

Oddly, given the amount of music in the score (the finale was the "United Nations Hymn," which was sung by Grayson to the accompaniment of an army orchestra), Kelly only got to dance once, as a private soldier ordered to clean out his barracks, but instead aiming his mop at a portrait of Adolf Hitler as though it were a machine-gun. This was the first of those ground-breaking Kelly dances in which his solo steps were coordinated with an inanimate object, in this case the mop, almost like a duet. One moment he's mopping the floor, the next he's dancing, and even a split second of inattention will make you miss the moment of transition from one to the other.

This was Kelly's special genius, the ability to make anything dance in character. As he explained: "I realized that there was no character—whether a sailor or a truck driver or a gangster—that couldn't be interpreted through dancing, if one found the correct choreographic language. What you *can't* have is a truck driver coming on stage and doing an *entrechat*. Because that would be incongruous, like a lady opening her mouth and singing bass. But there was a way of getting that truck driver to dance that would *not* be incongruous —just as there was a way of making Harry the Hoofer, a saloon bum, look convincing."

Thousands Cheer was to be one of the top money-making musicals of the year and the *New York Herald Tribune* went so far as to say that Kelly "...dominated the film and saves the picture from being merely a parade of personalities."

By now, several months after Pearl Harbor, Gene was desperate to leave the studio and go on active service but MGM, realizing how much it now needed him, had little difficulty in persuading the authorities that a thirty-year-old actor could do more for the war effort by continuing to entertain and raise money for war bonds with frequent personal appearances all over the United States. The trouble was that, like a dog in a manger, MGM knew it wanted Kelly around but was frequently

RIGHT *With Lucille Ball in MGM's unhappy treatment of Cole Porter's Broadway hit* Dubarry Was a Lady. ☆

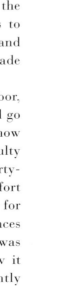

unable to decide what for. After *Thousands Cheer* he went straight into a drama called *The Cross of Lorraine*, a propaganda prison picture about a group of disparate characters who join the French army at the outbreak of war, only to be captured by the Nazis. Taking second billing to Jean-Pierre Aumont, Gene played a defeatist internee who is driven to join the Resistance and burn his own village to prevent it being useful to the Germans.

Given the fiasco over his Scottish dialect for *The Keys of the Kingdom*, Gene was relieved to discover that he would not have to acquire any kind of accent for the French soldier, any more than he had for the Italian-American in *Pilot Number 5*. He was a dancing actor, he decided, not a dramatic one. Other stars included Sir Cedric Hardwicke, Hume Cronyn, and Peter Lorre as a joke Nazi. Though the film opened to respectful reviews, the American public was already beginning to tire of war movies and box-office returns were not good.

What these recent films proved, at least to Gene's satisfaction, was that he was a draw in musicals but not in dramatic roles (although, later in his career, he was to develop into a notable straight actor and director). He begged MGM to find him another musical vehicle or, failing that, to allow him to join the Navy. Mayer responded that he had lost quite

enough of his prize assets to the armed services, but he added that while he still didn't have another suitable musical he was prepared to lend Gene to RKO, which was just starting pre-production on *Cover Girl*.

Though by no means the greatest of Hollywood musicals, this was to prove a crucial turning-point in Kelly's career. For the first time in Hollywood he was hired not only as the star, albeit with second billing to Rita Hayworth, but also as the movie's choreographer. Apart from its wonderful score by Jerome Kern and Ira Gershwin, the breakthrough here was that the dancing came directly out of the dramatic action instead of being a mere interruption. This followed the innovations introduced by Agnes de Mille, whose dances for the stage version of *Oklahoma!* had first been unleashed on Broadway in the previous year. These had changed the landscape of show dancing and paved the way for Gene to develop in film terms in the direction she had set. Not for the first time he was cast as the owner of a seedy nightclub, on this occasion in love with one of his dancing girls (Rita Hayworth). The part of Danny McGuire was not, however, won for Kelly without a great deal of difficulty. "As far as I was concerned," the producer, Arthur Schwartz, recalled, "there was only one man in Hollywood who could play the part and that

was Gene Kelly. But each time I mentioned this to Harry Cohn, the Columbia chief, he would explode."

"That tough Irishman with his tough Irish mug?" Cohn had said. "You must be joking. You couldn't put him in the same frame as my Rita. Forget it. Nothing doing. Besides, I saw him in *Pal Joey* and he is too goddamn short." Finally shooting began without a leading man and Schwartz, behind Cohn's back, negotiated with MGM for four weeks of Gene's time. Expecting fireworks at best and a firing at worst, he plucked up his courage and told Cohn. All Cohn said was "Thank God."

But even after Gene got there it wasn't smooth sailing, since Rita was in the midst of a stormy relationship with Orson Welles, whom she married during the filming. By then Cohn had reversed himself so totally and become so keen on the Kelly/Hayworth partnership, that he promised them the film version of *Pal Joey*. Sadly, that took another fifteen years to reach the screen and, by the time it did, Rita Hayworth's Joey was Frank Sinatra and she herself was playing the older role, with Kim Novak now the young girl.

Despite its wonderful score, *Cover Girl*, like so many musicals of the time, had a truly terrible script about a nightclub dancer who runs away to become a model, as her grandmother had done before her, but returns

LEFT *Playing a private soldier in MGM's all-star* Thousands Cheer, *Gene dances with a mop. This was the first instance of his brilliant use of inanimate objects as dancing partners.* ☆

when she realizes that love is more important than success. Rita, despite the traumas of her private life, had never looked happier on screen, dancing around vast circular ramps with her dress billowing out and the orchestra playing romantic arpeggios. Required to sing one song in a British accent, she went to Gracie Fields (then living in Los Angeles) for careful instruction. As a result, the song at least achieved a mid-Atlantic status with the emphasis on Lancashire vowels.

The musical highlight, though, was "Long Ago and Far Away," one of Kern's all-time classics, sung by Gene to Rita, and at the end of the film Kern sent Gene a plaque which read, simply, "To G.K. who is O.K. with J.K.," a recognition by Kern that Gene had been right to insist on cuts to some of the songs. But, undoubtedly, *Cover Girl* will live in musical-movie history for one dance, choreographed by Kelly and his young friend, Stanley Donen, and grown wholesale from Gene's imagination: the "alter-ego" sequence. Now recognized as one of the seminal dances in film musicals, it begins with Gene walking the streets of Brooklyn late at night and suddenly seeing his reflection in a shop window. He dances with his own reflection in a *doppelgänger* routine that ends with the reflection being destroyed and Kelly walking away alone.

Talking of his work on *Cover Girl*, Kelly said: "The trouble with Hollywood musicals at that time was that far too many of them still looked like photographs of Broadway hits. I was desperate to do things on the screen that simply could not be done in the theater.... it's a matter of fitting a three-dimensional art into a two-dimensional medium and there is nothing easy about it: everything works against you and I certainly couldn't have done "alter ego" without Stanley Donen, who would call out all the timings. We worked for a month on that dance, shot it in four days, and then spent a great deal more time editing all the double-printed footage. Having been told that technically the double-image could not be done, I was delighted to bring it off."

Clearly, this was the dance that influenced the title number for *Singin' in the Rain* eight years later. Similarly the "Make Way for Tomorrow" routine which Kelly performs with Hayworth and Phil Silvers was exactly the kind of exuberant trio that would reach glorious perfection throughout *On the Town*, five years later. In March, 1944, to round off Gene's triumph as the star/choreographer of *Cover Girl*, came the review from the *New York Herald Tribune*: "Whether he is forwarding the very slight romantic plot or merely tapping the daylights out of an ornamental set, Kelly is credible and immensely entertaining."

LEFT *Gene rehearses with Rita Hayworth on the set of* Cover Girl, *watched by director Charles Vidor and, at the piano, Phil Silvers.* ☆

6. Fred and the Follies

By the time *Cover Girl* was released MGM had finally understood what it had got in Kelly, and for the next fourteen years and twenty-one films he was never to work again for any other studio. However, in the period between the shooting and the release of *Cover Girl*, Metro continued to loan him out, this time to Universal for Robert Siodmak's remarkable and very under-rated movie *Christmas Holiday*.

> *"As a Depression kid who went to school in very bad years, I didn't want to move or dance like a rich man. I wanted to do the dance of the Proletariat, the movements of the people. I wanted to dress in a sailor suit or a pair of jeans. That was part of my social outlook"*
>
> **GENE KELLY**

RIGHT *A script conference during the shooting of* Anchors Aweigh, *directed by George Sidney, which included Gene's innovative and now classic dance with a cartoon mouse. Left to right: Sidney, Jerry, Gene, Tom.* ☆

The screenplay was based very loosely on a Somerset Maugham short story, and Deanna Durbin, who got top billing, was allowed to sing a couple of classic numbers: Frank Loesser's "Spring Will Be a Little Late This Year" and Irving Berlin's "Always." Kelly was cast as a psychopathic murderer and he played the role as slightly homosexual, which was an interesting effect and went some way toward disguising the fact that Durbin, as his wife, was having trouble making the transition to grown-up roles. Gene didn't care for the script, but his sense of patriotism told him not to complain. In time of war, he thought, if he couldn't be in the service himself, the least he could do was to take what was offered and regard it as a sort of duty. And as if to prove him wrong in his own estimation of the movie, *Christmas Holiday* was one of the most popular films of 1944.

By the time *Christmas Holiday* was in the can, MGM had lined up Gene's next musical, the one that was destined to bring him home to the studio in triumph. This was *Anchors Aweigh*, the story of two sailors (Kelly and Frank Sinatra) who spend their shore leave in Hollywood among the movie colony, which had promised to give their brave boys a good time. Gene still got only third billing, here to Sinatra and Kathryn Grayson; other stars included a young Dean Stockwell and the by

now inevitable José Iturbi, who was performing this time a boogie-woogie version of "The Donkey Serenade."

The score was the work of Sammy Cahn and Jule Styne and although Sinatra and Grayson got the best of it, Kelly had three major dances—"The Mexican Hat Dance," with little Sharon McManus, and an amazing fandango that had him leaping over parapets and making a 45-foot jump from a rooftop to the balcony of his beloved in full Fairbanks tradition. But the third of these dances became a great classic and the one that we think of whenever Kelly comes to mind.

It was the first ever dance to combine live action with animation, as the sailor Kelly teaches the bad-tempered Jerry (of *Tom and Jerry* fame) to dance. And it was entirely Gene's idea. The four minutes of screen time involved 10,000 painted frames to synchronize with Kelly's movements. After devising a meticulous storyboard, Kelly was filmed doing his part of the sequence then the mouse was animated frame by frame before the two figures were optically linked. The cartoon sequence took two months to complete and was again born out of Kelly's desire to do something on film that could not be done on stage and had never been done before.

"Stanley Donen and I sat around for a couple of days trying to think of something.

RIGHT *Although Kathryn Grayson and Frank Sinatra headed the bill,* Anchors Aweigh *won Gene his first Oscar nomination as Best Actor.* ☆

and after one long period of silence Stanley suddenly said: "How about dancing with a cartoon?" That was it. The MGM brass didn't think it could be done but Joe Pasternak, our producer, went to bat for us and he got us a budget of $100,000 to make it as an independent production, warning us that very probably it would not appear in the movie at all. Stanley and I went to Walt Disney, to get his advice and possibly hire some of his men to work for us. But this wasn't possible because the Disney studio was so busy it couldn't accept any extra work. Disney was himself experimenting with live action and animation at that time, although he had nothing as difficult in mind as what we hoped to do. But he gave us his blessing, and the fact that Disney considered the idea feasible helped us to persuade the MGM cartoon department to do the job. I get all the credit for this, but it would have been impossible for me without Stanley Donen. He worked with the cameraman and called the shots in all the intricate timings and movements. It sure wasn't easy for the cameraman: he was being asked to photograph something that wasn't there."

Stanley Donen remembers a slightly more uneasy encounter with Disney. "'Mickey Mouse,' he told us, 'does not work for MGM.' That's how Jerry Mouse got the job."

All over America *Anchors Aweigh* broke box-office records and established Kelly at last as a star with a distinctly innovative and often revolutionary cinematic style. It also won him his first Academy Award nomination as Best Actor, as well as a Best Picture nomination for Joe Pasternak. The citation from the Academy read: "Gene Kelly's innovation in film dancing has done more than anything else in many years to yank movie musicals out of their accustomed rut." In the event, however, Best Actor went to Ray Milland for *The Lost Weekend*, which also brought home the Best Picture statue.

It seemed at that time that whenever MGM ran out of ideas for new musicals it made a tribute to the legendary showman-impresario, Florenz Ziegfeld. With two already on the shelves, *The Great Ziegfeld* from 1936 and the 1941 *Ziegfeld Girl*, it was decided that what the great American public wanted was, yes, another celebration of Ziegfeld, and *Ziegfeld Follies* became Gene's next assignment. It was a huge Technicolor blow-out but is notable mainly for giving Gene the only opportunity in his career (except for a bit of softshoe on the introductions to the 1976 *That's Entertainment II*) to dance with Fred Astaire.

Everyone in Hollywood had a Fred Astaire/Gene Kelly joke and the general assumption, studiously denied by both, was of a great rivalry. "Every time Gene Kelly starts dancing, Fred Astaire starts counting his money," Bob Hope said on one occasion while, on another, the critic Richard Schikel memorably remarked: "If Fred Astaire was white tie and tails, Gene Kelly is white socks and loafers." Even Gene himself got into the act: "If Fred Astaire is the Cary Grant of dance, I'm the Marlon Brando." But it was the critic Arlene Croce who nailed the comparison best. "The major difference between Astaire and Kelly is a difference not of talent or technique, but of levels of sophistication.... Kelly is not a winged dancer, he's a hoofer and more earthbound, but as an actor he has warmth and range.... His acting is slightly larger than life and he leaps into a simple scene distinctively eager and with a chesty, athletic, over-dramatic exuberance that makes audiences feel good."

That's a dance critic's point of view. Pauline Kael was a film critic and she was therefore more inclined to look for the emotional comparisons. "...Astaire is impervious to emotion, no matter what calamity he has to face ... whereas Kelly is a suffering human being ... Kelly bleeds and Astaire doesn't because Astaire ... is a great stick figure ... He is not a man who suffers, but a dancer who does things through stylized dance. Kelly, on the other hand, is a hoofer

LEFT *The climax of Ziegfeld Follies (1946) was "The Babbitt and the Bromide," a rare duet between Gene Kelly and Fred Astaire.* ☆

who .... brings a freshness to his line-readings which no song-and-dance man has done before, and his voice is a beautiful emotional instrument." Clive Hirschhorn has said that: "Astaire's breathtaking routines were rubies, emeralds and diamonds in scripts constructed out of paste.... Gene's dance routines, on the other hand, sprang naturally from the plot."

The two men—constantly compared by a show-business press ever eager to place one above the other or to discern signs of jealousy —were in fact acquaintances at most. They never quarreled but they really only ever met at public Hollywood celebrations. And, as Gene said: "The fact is that Fred and myself were in no way similar, nor even the best male dancers around. There were ballet dancers vastly superior to both of us but they of course never reached our mass audiences, so Fred and I got the cream of the publicity and naturally we were compared.

"While I personally was proud of the comparison, because there was no one to touch Fred when it came to popular dance, we felt that the film critics of the time should have made more of an effort to differentiate between our two styles. Fred and I both got very edgy when our names were mentioned in the same breath. My approach was completely different from his and we wanted the world not to lump us together like peas in a pod. If we had any resentment, it was not with each other but with the journalists who talked about two highly individual dancers as if they were one person. For instance, the sort of wardrobe I wore—blue jeans, sweatshirt, sneakers—Fred would never have been caught dead in. He was always immaculate at rehearsals, while I was always in an old shirt. Fred's steps were small, neat, graceful and intimate where mine were ballet-oriented and very athletic. We were never rivals. And although when Fred announced his retirement in 1946 there were people who thought he no longer wanted to compete with 'the new boy' nothing was further from the truth. Fred was still at the height of his powers, and the only reason for his retirement was that he was so saddened by the death of his first wife he felt he no longer wanted to work. Two years later I was the one who persuaded him to put on his dancing shoes again and replace me in *Easter Parade* after I had broken my ankle; if we had been rivals I certainly wouldn't have encouraged him to make a comeback."

That may indeed have been true, and Astaire too private a person to admit that his grief was the reason for his retirement. But what he actually said at the time was: "My style no longer matches the contemporary mood and I see Gene Kelly now gaining the admiration that greeted me ten years earlier."

RIGHT *The Gershwins' "The Babbitt and the Bromide" was Astaire's choice of material but better suited to Gene's style of dancing. They would not appear together again for another thirty years.* ☆

Around this time, in March 1946, *Ziegfeld Follies* was released. It was a deliberate and glossy throwback to the kind of all-star, all-singing, all-dancing Broadway stage revues which had flourished before the war but were by now already a thing of the past. To introduce it, the actor William Powell reappeared from his 1936 *The Great Ziegfeld*, but speaking to us now from a luxurious penthouse apartment in Heaven. There he dreams about a new show and makes a list of possible stars ... whereupon Fred Astaire appears, back on earth, to speak his own tribute to Ziegfeld, thereby cueing in Powell's fantasy revue.

There then followed twelve sketches or musical numbers, of which the best were Lucille Ball as the circus ringmistress "Bringing on the Beautiful Girls;" the inevitable Esther Williams water ballet; several vaudeville sketches; Fred Astaire dancing with Lucille Bremer to "Limehouse Blues;" Judy Garland doing a wicked parody of Greer Garson giving an interview, in a savage sketch written by Kay Thompson; and, as a climax to the show, Fred and Gene dancing and singing "The Babbitt and the Bromide," a song which Fred and his sister, Adele, had originally performed in the 1927 Broadway musical *Funny Face* by George and Ira Gershwin.

This is a curiously Anglophile number in which a couple of club bores meet at intervals in their lives only to address the same clichés to each other ("Hello, how are you? Howzafolks? What's new?") and a whole outpouring of similarly pointless comments, none of which the other man can ever recall. Although the number really only repeats the same point about the inanity of catchphrases for verse after verse until at the last the two end up in Heaven with no improvement in their conversation, Ira was delighted to note that his lyric was the first ever to be honored by inclusion in the *American Anthology of Light Verse.*

Considering that there was not to be another appearance together on screen by Fred and Gene for some forty years, their choice of material here was more than a little disappointing. Indeed, Gene never wanted to do it at all, preferring a Red Indian number by Blane and Martin called "Pass that Peace Pipe." In a surfeit of professional politeness and with more than a touch of "No, no, after you, Alfonse," Fred graciously ceded the choice to Gene who, when he heard of it, immediately insisted that of course they would do the number Fred wanted. But this gentlemanly difference of opinion between the two greatest dancers in the history of Hollywood was to simmer on for years. In a

1950 interview Gene said he had been deeply uncomfortable in the number because his style was so different from Fred's. He thought he looked "like a klutz" and wished their one dance together had not been so light and unchallenging. Hearing of this, Fred sharply responded: "What does he mean by unchallenging? Didn't we beat the hell out of that floor together? We were supposed to be a popular team. We weren't trying, after all, to do *L'Après Midi d'un Faun.*"

In fact, the freedom of the dance's choreography is much better suited to Gene's athletic style than to Fred's smaller, more precise footwork and, if contest it is, Gene wins. It was staged by Vincente Minnelli, who would never really be drawn on the relationship between the two giants on the set, who circled each other with exaggerated courtesy. "It was quite, quite fascinating to watch," was all he would say.

Gene was more forthcoming: "The thing I remember most plainly about The Babbitt and the Bromide was the rehearsals. Of course Fred was the senior partner and if I felt there was any conflict or any doubt about any step I would certainly defer to him, but he made it so there wasn't any. I never worked with a gentler or nicer man. That isn't to say Fred isn't very tough. He can be hard as nails, and I've seen him be that way, but only because he wants

RIGHT Lieutenant Kelly. Gene's enlistment in the Navy in late 1944 eventually led to documentary film-making and editing experience that proved invaluable. ☆

his dances as good as they can be. Fred felt happy about this number because he had done it years before with his sister, Adele".

Minnelli received sole directing credit on *Ziegfeld Follies*, but so ambitious was the project and so slow the production (started in the May of 1944, it would not be released until the spring of 1946) that five other directors, including George Sidney and Charles Walters, came in for various numbers. The official choreography credit went to Gene's mentor, Robert Alton, but there is no doubt of Kelly's involvement there, too. Roger Edens was in charge of the music; Lena Horne's husband, Lennie Hayton, was the conductor; and of all the musicals to have emerged from the Arthur Freed unit at MGM, this was reckoned if not the best then certainly the most ambitious.

By the time shooting ended on *Ziegfeld Follies* it was November 1944, and with the war showing no sign of ending, Gene finally persuaded MGM to let him enlist in the Navy. He was sent to boot camp in San Diego for thirteen weeks.

7. Porter and "The Pirate"

In the eighteen months between the shooting and the first release of *Ziegfeld Follies*, Gene had been into and out of the United States Navy. Hitherto, the closest he had come to the war was the somewhat trite *Pilot Number 5* but his determination to see real action led him, courtesy of Louis B. Mayer's still grudging release, to thirteen tough weeks in San Diego being taught how to kill. Kelly was appalled by the experience: shocked by the way he and the other new recruits were dehumanized, and horrified by the regimentation of being told when to get up, when to eat, and when to turn out the lights. He later told Clive Hirschhorn that it was "like living in a police state and absolute anathema to my philosophy of life—but this was war and there was precious little I could do about it."

> "His fierce urge for perfection, his almost fanatical need for success, have always been matched by his need for justice for the less gifted, or less advantaged, whose paths crossed his. Gene climbed to the top but he didn't step on any hearts on the way up"
>
> FRANK SINATRA

RIGHT *This exuberant dance with a statue is one of the Kelly-inspired highlights of the otherwise dire* Living in a Big Way. ☆

After training, the new Lieutenant Junior Grade was assigned to the Navy Photographic Service as a cameraman. There were mutterings from the other inductees about his cushy job, but his only real regret was that they hadn't properly trained him to make his films to a higher standard. Among his tasks was a documentary intended as a morale-boosting exercise, "to demonstrate the benefits of a new experimental fire-fighting foam." Always the perfectionist, Kelly hated doing the job badly and he was never taught how to do it better. This didn't stop the Navy sending him next to a newly commissioned naval cruiser, the USS *Fall River*, with instructions to make a detailed photographic survey, again without sufficient training or equipment.

But for Kelly, as for everyone else, life changed drastically with the dropping of the first atom bomb on Hiroshima on August 6th, 1945. At that moment Kelly was actually on his way to a planned raid on Japan. His ship was stopped at Hawaii and ordered to return to San Francisco to await new orders.

Although peace was imminent, there was still much to do. He went first to the Submarine Service to make a propaganda film, the purpose of which was to demonstrate that submarine life did not have to be claustrophobic. What the Navy didn't know when it sent him under water was that he himself was a claustrophobic. Accustomed as a dancer to space and light, the submarine life was for Gene pure hell. But his last two assignments for the Navy, though he could hardly have known this at the time, were to prove invaluable to his future career. The first of these was to shoot a documentary about the survivors of the USS *Benjamin Franklin* after it had been the victim of kamikaze attacks. The location was the Brooklyn Naval Yard, where he spent a week (and where he would return in 1950 at his insistence, to shoot his classic, *On the Town*).

The second and last assignment of his service life in the winter of 1945–6 was to edit the *Navy Screen Magazine*, a weekly film round-up of newsreel footage thought to be of special interest to those still serving at sea. Once again, his first experience of editing was to come in more than useful after his discharge in May, 1946, and for the rest of his life.

Kelly's return to Hollywood was nothing to write home about. On the family front, with Kerry now approaching school age, his wife, Betsy Blair, had returned to her own acting career. Though she was always to remain, on stage and screen, a character actress rather than a star, her films over the next five years (*A Double Life, Another Part of the Forest, The Snakepit*, and *Marty*) were to be at least

as notable as, and often a lot more so than, those made by her husband in these often difficult and unrewarding post-war years.

But the marriage was still very strong and they decided to invest all their worldly wealth (some $37,000) in what they reckoned was the last surviving Beverly Hills farmhouse. This left them without a penny for decorating but, as Gene was suddenly to find himself with more spare time on his hands than he had ever feared or expected, this proved not to be a problem. While Betsy filmed, he did the decorating and was relieved to discover that, though it appeared not to have the faintest idea of what to do with him, MGM had agreed to restore him to his full salary, having only paid a small fraction of it during his wartime service.

The year 1946 was the year in which Hollywood reached an all-time high. Some 500 films were released to 20,000 cinemas across America; 600 actors were on full-time studio contracts; with the average ticket price at forty cents, ninety million people went to the movies at least once a week. Judy Garland, the top box-office star of the year, was earning $6,000 a week while Marilyn Monroe in her first contract was only on $100. Apart from Garland, the other nine top stars of the time were, in order: Bing Crosby, Ingrid Bergman, Van Johnson, Gary Cooper, Bob Hope,

Humphrey Bogart, Greer Garson, Betty Grable and Roy Rogers.

This was the studio world to which Kelly returned but it soon became painfully clear that there was no obvious place in it for him. One of the problems was that his image so far had been inextricably linked to war films: five out of the eight pictures he had made since arriving in California showed him in uniform. The other great problem was that with the return from the services of MGM's senior leading men (Clark Gable, James Stewart, Robert Taylor, Van Heflin and Robert Montgomery), Kelly's rank on the studio roster inevitably sank to about seventh.

But his greatest humiliation was yet to come. MGM, still owning half his contract and paying his weekly salary, forced him into a dire comedy, *Living in a Big Way*, designed to promote Marie "The Body" McDonald. Amazingly, even though it already had Marilyn Monroe under contract, the studio had mysteriously decided that Miss McDonald was to be its next big sex symbol. Her movie career was to be brief and inglorious and there is considerable evidence to suggest that Louis B. Mayer's interest in her was something other than professional. Kelly himself was memorably to describe her as the original triple threat: "She could neither sing nor dance nor act." All the same, he was obliged

ABOVE *With (left to right) Jane Wyman, Henry Fonda, Ronald Reagan and Boris Karloff at a meeting of the Screen Actors Guild during the labour strike in 1946.* ☆

LEFT *Still in uniform, Gene enjoys an evening out with Betsy at the Waldorf, Christmas 1945.* ☆

not only to be her co-star but to devise four dance numbers uneasily interpolated into the script. One of these has him and a halting McDonald dancing to "It Had To Be You." The other three were only added after the studio realised the extent of the trouble it was in with the apparently finished film. These, therefore, are mercifully McDonald-free zones and although the film is long since lost, no less a choreographer than Martha Graham suggested that they represented Gene's best work.

The first of these, "Fido and Me," has him dancing with an amazingly well-trained dog, while the second gives him as partner a large female statue which, like the dog, was an altogether more animated dancer than Miss McDonald. But it is in the third dance that we see for the first time the direction in which Kelly was going both as dancer and as choreographer. It lasts for no more than four minutes of screen time but is built around a series of children's games and set in a half-completed apartment building.

Apart from these brief pointers to his future, *Living in a Big Way* was, like the whole of 1946, to prove a nightmare for Kelly. In the middle of shooting, the unions, flexing their postwar muscles, and aware that MGM in particular was still being run like a prewar dictatorship, declared an all-out labor strike. Gene, a junior and recent addition to the

board of directors of the Screenwriters' Guild, was sent to the union's head office in Chicago to negotiate a fair settlement. This he did, and was inevitably then branded by Hollywood's far right as a dangerous pro-labor radical; in fact, he was nothing of the kind, he had just got the best deal he could that was acceptable to both sides. Back in Hollywood, just when it looked as though MGM had finally got him back in its view-finder and was offering him the chance to co-star with Judy Garland in *Easter Parade*, Kelly went out one evening to play volleyball with a group of kids from his neighborhood and, catastrophically, broke his ankle. Terrified of telling Mayer the truth lest this should prove a contract-ending offense, he merely told his boss that he had damaged himself while rehearsing a complex *Easter Parade* dance routine. Mayer, with the film already underway, was beside himself with anxiety and asked Gene what the hell they should do now. Kelly's reply was simple, to the point and only three words long. "I'll call Fred."

Astaire duly came out of retirement at Gene's request to take over the role that might, all other things being equal, have re-established Kelly at last. Instead, Gene was left to take Betsy on a rueful European holiday and then, while still technically unemployed, to deal with a whole new Hollywood problem

that landed dangerously close to his own doorstep. Because of his involvement a few months earlier in the union dispute, Kelly was now regarded with some suspicion. Moreover, Betsy had been politically committed for some time to an active involvement in anti-fascist committees, an interest which was to do serious harm to her career. In a Hollywood already spooked by the union uprising, anti-Communism was the prevailing wisdom while fascism, a concern on the East Coast and in Europe, was really too far from California to have made many inroads into the consciousness of the film community.

By the summer of 1947 a congressman and former insurance broker called J. Parnell Thomas was already holding public hearings on behalf of the House Un-American Activities Committee. Kelly, his ankle still in plaster, joined the group of twenty-seven Hollywood rebels—led by John Huston, William Wyler, Humphrey Bogart, Lauren Bacall, and Danny Kaye—who flew to Washington DC to confront the Committee, a confrontation which ended tragically in the the arrest of the "Unfriendly Ten." But the HUAC had nothing on Kelly who, asked soon afterward by the American Legion whether he was or had ever been Communist, said that all his life he had loathed anything, including this, which smacked of any kind of regimentation. "I am simply a liberal who believes in the freedom of the artist and therefore cannot stand by while the careers of those I love and admire are being destroyed by a senseless purge. The only line I have ever known how to follow is the American line."

It is some measure of Kelly's honorable stature, even at this low ebb in his professional fortunes, that his answer (unlike those of many others speaking in similar vein) was accepted unconditionally even by those furthest to the right of him and Betsy. In later years Kelly would say that his own career and, to a much greater extent, that of his wife, had been damaged by these proto-McCarthyite smears; and yet, within a month or two of his return to Hollywood, he was offered the film that would restore his fortunes.

The Pirate was to give him a wonderful crack at the full Fairbanks/Flynn kind of swashbuckler, but with the songs and dances that they could never even have thought about, let alone performed. It was both a homage to and a parody of the vintage period romances that Gene was later to mock again, affectionately, in the costume section of *Singin' in the Rain*.

The script of *The Pirate* had a curious and contorted history. It had started as a 1911 German stage comedy, *Der Seeräuber*, about a notorious pirate becoming the mayor of a respectable island in the Caribbean. In 1943

ABOVE *The five-year-old Kerry Kelly inspects the broken ankle that cost Gene his part in MGM's* Easter Parade. ☆

the Broadway playwright S.N. Behrman had turned it into a hit for Alfred Lunt and Lynn Fontanne, building in a wandering actor who impersonates the pirate in order to win the hand of a young girl.

Vincente Minnelli, then married to Judy Garland, saw the play and suggested to Arthur Freed that it would be a fine vehicle for his wife. They persuaded Cole Porter to write the score and thus it was that *The Pirate* became the MGM musical of 1948. Now, almost fifty years later, the film, like so many of its originally misunderstood kind, has become a cult classic for festivals and retrospectives; at the time, however, it had its problems.

For a start, Gene seriously doubted his ability to get back to the top of his form. As he lugubriously told the *Los Angeles Times* during the first week of shooting: "Two years in the Navy, three years off the screen, I shall never be the dancer I was. I put on eighteen pounds in the Navy and I am only just working them off. Besides, I am a lot older now than when I made *Cover Girl* and *Anchors Aweigh*. With Fred Astaire already retiring, I do start to wonder how much longer I've got. Besides, I was a much better dancer when I first got to Broadway than I am now. I was younger, that's why. A dancer is like a prizefighter. He gets superannuated very early; can't take it nearly so well in his thirties." He was just

thirty-six and all his greatest films were still ahead of him.

Gene later described *The Pirate* as one of his most rewarding professional experiences, with tremendous support from his producer, director, and co-star. All the same, shooting did not get off to a very good start. Judy, already attended on set by one of her many resident psychiatrists, was in her usual state of private and professional trauma, not helped now by the fact that her marriage to Minnelli was already on the rocks, despite the recent birth of their daughter, Liza.

Shooting started on *The Pirate* just after St Valentine's Day in 1947 but on the second day, gossip columnist Hedda Hopper found Judy in her dressing room "shaking like an aspen leaf and in a frenzy of hysteria, claiming that all who loved her had now turned against her and were tapping her telephone calls." One of the many writers of *The Pirate*, Anita Loos, later wrote: "I recall an early day at the studio when mild little Vincente Minnelli was waiting to direct Judy in one of the big scenes. As usual she was late for work, and everybody, including Kelly, Gladys Cooper, and 150 extras had been marking time since eight in the morning. Finally, at noon, Vincente was summoned to the phone to learn that Judy required him to get home at once and escort her to an ice-cream parlour for a soda."

RIGHT *The finishing touches are put to Gene's dastardly look for* The Pirate, *Vincente Minnelli's sophisticated musical parody of the vintage swashbuckler.* ☆

With all Judy's problems, by June the film was, not surprisingly, only half-finished but already almost a million dollars over budget. When they finally reached Kelly's pirate ballet in mid-August *The Pirate* had taken 135 days to film, for 99 of which Judy had been absent. But Garland was still magic and together she and Gene transcended their material. Pauline Kael wrote about this most important of Gene's partnerships: "In Garland alone did Kelly find a female counterpart. She joined her odd and undervalued cake-walker's prance to his large-spirited hoofing, and he joined his odd, light, high voice to her sweet deep one."

The Pirate was the most strenuous and sophisticated movie that either Gene or Judy had ever attempted. It required virtuoso acting, dervish dancing, and the mastery of a volatile, lusty Cole Porter score of which the highlight was only added as an afterthought once the principal photography had been completed. This was the knockabout "Be A Clown," a number that Judy and Gene begged for and finally got, which became *the* hit of the film. Gene did all his own stunts, including a pirate ballet that required him to swing from balcony to balcony in time with pre-recorded music, ending up always on the right foot and poised for the next choreographic movement.

The plot was byzantine even in the original German play, so by the time it had been

rewritten by Behrman for Broadway, then by Joe Mankiewicz, Anita Loos, and Joseph Than for the movie, it was well-nigh incomprehensible. At the readthrough it was rejected with some hilarity by almost all of the powerful cast, which included Walter Slezak, Gladys Cooper and, best of all from Gene's point of view, the Nicholas Brothers. It was then handed on to the wonderfully named husband-and-wife rewrite team of Albert Hackett and Frances Goodrich, who had made their reputation with the best of the Nelson Eddy/Jeanette MacDonald musicals some fifteen years earlier.

Plot complexities notwithstanding, Gene had little to complain about except for the idiotic curls that the makeup department imposed on his receding hairline. Arthur Freed, now at the height of his MGM power, was dedicated to turning choreographers into directors and he gave Gene the chance to direct his own dances (with Robert Alton) and reunited him with the best musical team in the business: vocal arrangements were by Kay Thompson, Roger Edens and Robert Tucker; the conductor was Lennie Hayton; and the orchestrations were by Conrad Salinger. Apart from the pirate ballet, "Be A Clown," and "Nina" (a savage little Porter satire on Ravel's "Bolero"), the highlight of the film was undoubtedly Kelly's dancing with the innovative and amazingly athletic Nicholas Brothers. But even this was trouble, as the sight of a white man teaming up with black dancers cost the film several bookings in the southern states.

All the same, throughout the retakes, editing and final dubbing Kelly, Freed and Minnelli all thought they had made a masterpiece. Only Cole Porter, with his more cynical but alert awareness of what an audience wanted at that time, had his doubts, and when the film was released, early in 1948, it was old king Cole who, as usual, had got it right.

In later life Freed felt they had made the film either twenty years too late or twenty years too early; the postwar public were not sufficiently acquainted with the work of Douglas Fairbanks Sr. and John Barrymore to understand this loving parody, while those who were old enough resented having their heroes lampooned.

The early reviews were terrible. A few years later it was Gene who precisely pinpointed the problem. "After the previews Vincente and I honestly believed we were being so dazzlingly brilliant and clever that everybody would fall at our feet and swoon away in delight and ecstasy as they kissed each of our toes in appreciation for this wondrous new musical that we had given them. Boy, were we wrong.

ABOVE *On an MGM backlot Gene brushes up his tightrope walking for a key moment in The Pirate.* ☆

RIGHT *Gene makes it to Judy Garland's quarters, and with brio, but Minnelli's affectionate homage to Douglas Fairbanks Sr failed to strike a chord with the postwar public.* ☆

About five and a half people seemed to get the gist of what we had set out to do, and in retrospect you really couldn't blame any of the others. We just didn't pull it off. Not completely. Whatever I did just looked like fake Barrymore and phony Fairbanks. That was the result of the damned elusive camera, which I had been trying so hard to tame. It all looked just wonderful in rehearsal. The sophisticates grasped it, but the film died in the hinterlands. It was done tongue in cheek and I should have realized that never really works. But I still thought Judy, for all her troubles, was superb and what Minnelli did with color and design in that film is just as fine as anything that has ever been done."

The last word on it should probably go to the greatest American film critic writing at the time of its initial release, James Agee: "*The Pirate* has the death's head, culture-cute mirthful grin of your average Shakespearean comic and is ultimately about as unfunny. As an all-out try at artful movie-making, this is among the most interesting pictures of the year. Unhappily, most of the very considerable artistry that Kelly has put into this production collides head-on with artiness or is spoiled by simpler kinds of miscalculation."

8. D'Artagnan to Donen

Although the eventual box-office figures on *The Pirate* gave MGM a reasonable return on its investment—total cost: $2,500,000; first-release gross: $6,800,000—the studio feeling was that the sooner Judy and Gene could return to less experimental material, the better. Accordingly, Gene was now cast as d'Artagnan in a routine 1948 remake of *The Three Musketeers* (no French accent

> ***"All for one, one for all"***
> ALEXANDRE DUMAS

required). One of the few unanswered questions that still hangs over the Kelly career is how good he would have been as a straight actor had he not primarily been a dancer-choreographer. It was, in this same year, Billy Wilder's idea to cast him in the William Holden role in *Sunset Boulevard*, but this was a contractual impossibility and it is only very occasionally in these musical years that one catches a glimpse of just how good Kelly could be as an actor. *The Three Musketeers* provides one such chance.

RIGHT *Swashbuckling Fairbanks-style is thirsty work: a welcome break during the shooting of* The Three Musketeers. ☆

Although there had been at least half a dozen previous American or European movies from the original Dumas classic novel (Don Ameche and the Ritz Brothers had even done it as a musical lampoon in 1939), this was to be by far the most expensive and ambitious. MGM put not only Kelly, Lana Turner, June Allyson, Vincent Price, and Angela Lansbury, but also nearly $3,000,000 (a near-record budget for a non-musical at the time) into a version which only really suffers from its inability to decide how seriously to take itself. The comrades in arms were Gig Young, Robert Coote and Van Heflin as Athos, Porthos and Aramis; Kelly, who as a boy had always idolized Fairbanks and was keen to follow in his movie-gymnast footsteps, was delighted to have inherited d'Artagnan from Douglas Sr.

Gene's one regret was that MGM had refused his inevitable request to make it as a musical. He contented his choreographer self with weeks of fencing practice in which he was partnered by Jean Heremens, a Belgian fencing world master, who taught him the routines and turned up in the film as various opponents. Gene's ballet training, he noted later, proved invaluable when it came to swordsmanship: "In both, the feet are always placed outward, making it possible to move quickly from side to side and to use your body to the full. Unless your toes were turned outward, period costumes made it very difficult to move easily in a duel. So when I first started fencing I had no problem in moving around but the difficulty was to train my reflexes to deflect with speed and then come back at my opponent.

"What I most envied about Fairbanks in the silent version was the way he would register his satisfaction after completing an especially dazzling trick, without ever being smug about it. There was just something in his expression that acknowledged his own excellence and it was very engaging. When I tried to acquire the same sort of nonchalance for my d'Artagnan, I was never able to be as ingenuous; with me it always came out taunting. Fairbanks had a combination of naiveté and arrogance which was unrivaled in the cinema. And although there was not a trick in his entire repertoire which I could not duplicate, the 'brio' with which he performed them was his and his alone." This remained, of all his non-musical films, Kelly's favorite, not least because when, some years later, he was on holiday in Ghana, he discovered that, after a screening of *The Three Musketeers* at the local cinema, he was a far greater star than a Russian female cosmonaut newly arrived in town from the Soviet space program.

Away from the studios Gene and Betsy were still making their Beverly Hills home a refuge

RIGHT *Gene and Betsy at their Beverly Hills Home on Rodeo Drive.* ☆

for European visitors and those local film people who found in their amiable liberalism a welcome change from what was still a very conservative industry (albeit a refuge demanding considerable energy, given that The Game was still a requirement of any evening at the Kellys').

One young visitor to Hollywood at this time was the critic Kenneth Tynan, who noted a subtle difference between evenings at George Cukor's house, another of the great welcoming salons for visiting Europeans, and those at Gene's and Betsy's. As Tynan's widow Kathleen was to note: "At the Kelly house on Rodeo Drive in the flats of Beverly Hills, the company was politically much more convivial than at Cukor's and more dismayingly intellectual. No guest, Ken said, lolled naked here on leopard-skin divans. Instead, the Kelly house was animated by the Pittsburgh-Irish host's competitive intelligence and charm and his then wife Betsy Blair's active support for left causes. Their front door was never locked and through it poured a talented bunch (mostly from New York) who would make their way straight to the bar. There was lively political talk, and noisy charades, and endless word games. There was usually someone at the piano, Leonard Bernstein or Oscar Levant, who would call out: 'What'll it be, kids? A "Stabat Mater" or a blues?' Judy Garland and

Lena Horne would sing while Marilyn Monroe made hot dogs."

"Ken so loved our gang," Gene recalled, "that when his then-girl, Elaine Dundy, had to leave Los Angeles, he moved in with us, writing in the mornings in the front room, looking out to the black acacia trees and the milky skies before the sun broke." Indeed, on one memorable night at Gene's, Ken met for the first time, and fell instantly in love with, a white-skinned, blue-eyed Dresden doll called Carol Saroyan. He spoke not a word to her until the evening broke up, whereupon he demanded of her: "Will you come to England tomorrow and marry me?" "Don't be so dumb," replied the Dresden doll. "Most days I can't even make it to the drugstore."

Michael Kidd was taken to the Kellys' on his first Saturday night in Hollywood and was thenceforth part of Gene's gang. "It was packed with people, everybody you could think of; every Saturday night the whole movie industry would go to Gene's house. He and his wife and daughter would even put on little acts for us and Gene was always busy tending the bar, greeting everybody, socializing; and the next morning he would be fit for that murderous volleyball game."

Gene needed all the energy his high-octane lifestyle was providing. At this time his great dream was to make the definitive film of

Cyrano de Bergerac. Edmund Rostand's play had never been filmed in English and it was to be another forty years before Gérard Depardieu would turn it into a film classic. In the meantime, the ever-thoughtful Louis B. Mayer told Kelly that just one false nose would be the ruin of his career and it was left to José Ferrer to make the picture two years later.

Sulking, Gene took his family on a skiing trip to Switzerland and on his return discovered that he had been drafted into *Words and Music*, MGM's all-singing, all-dancing (if wildly unbelievable) life of Richard Rodgers and Lorenz Hart, starring Tom Drake and Mickey Rooney. Again Gene was brought in to choreograph and dance, with Vera-Ellen, the "Slaughter on Tenth Avenue" number—originally staged on Broadway in 1937 by the ballet choreographer Georges Balanchine as a vehicle for Ray Bolger in the backstage musical *On Your Toes*. "I only had the one number in *Words and Music*," Gene recalled, "and I changed the libretto from the comedy which Balanchine had done for Ray Bolger to a tragic ballet. Of course, he had to do comedy for Bolger. We rehearsed the number for four weeks and shot it in three days." It was a sensation, the first complete ballet in a Hollywood film, and it vindicated everything that Kelly had been arguing for. Cinema audiences would indeed accept

modern ballet in filmic form, so long as it had the energy and pace to move the movie along rather than being merely an elegant interruption. This was film dance on its own terms.

But those looking for any kind of truth in the story of Rodgers and Hart would have to look elsewhere. Hart, already five years dead, had been a brilliantly gifted homosexual alcoholic. Mickey Rooney wasn't having any of that. Hart thus emerges as the sidekick to Tom Drake's Rodgers, a performance of breathtaking dullness which could well be attributed to the fact that Rodgers and his lawyers were keeping an extremely beady eye on every aspect of the footage. Hart's ghost merely had to contend with a Jewish-American gay being played by a five-times married Irish-American. Accordingly, Arthur Freed fell back on the format that had never failed him in times of real-life biographical trouble. He turned the whole picture into an all-star revue featuring not only Gene Kelly and Vera-Ellen but also Judy Garland, Lena Horne, June Allyson, Cyd Charisse and Mel Tormé, all of them singing or dancing Rodgers and Hart classics.

By now MGM had given up on finding Gene a regular dancing partner but it was still keen to cash in on his previous hits. Thus it was that after *Words and Music* it decided to

BELOW *Guest stars in*
Words and Music, *Gene
and Vera-Ellen perform
"Slaughter of Tenth
Avenue," the first use of
a complete ballet in a
Hollywood film.* ☆

reunite him with Frank Sinatra. But there was
just one little problem: nobody had the
faintest idea what to do for a script. The
producer Joe Pasternak had in his bottom
drawer a story about two sailors turning an
old aircraft carrier into a floating nightclub
but, as both Kelly and Sinatra pointed out, it
was the kind of screenplay that even Rooney
and Garland would have rejected. Gene
himself therefore started to write a screenplay,
as usual calling in Stanley Donen to help him
out. Neither was a screenwriter and all they
achieved was a two-page outline about a
couple of baseball players turning to
vaudeville at the turn of the century. Because
they were who they were, they managed to sell
this amorphous bit of paper for $25,000 to
Arthur Freed. He promptly called in two real
writers (Harry Tugend and George Wells) for
the script, Betty Comden and Adolph Green
for the lyrics, and Harold Arlen for the music,
while there were many additions from the
likes of Roger Edens and Yip Harburg. The
girlfriends were to be played by Betty Garrett
and a non-aquatic Esther Williams ("Wet she's
a star, dry she ain't." Anon.).

But most surprising of all was Freed's
choice of a director. Almost a decade after his
last real hits, and following considerable
alcoholic and other difficulties, Busby
Berkeley was chosen to make what sense he

RIGHT *On the set of* Take Me Out to the Ball Game, *Gene discusses with Busby Berkeley the next step in a bedroom sequence. A surprise choice as director, Berkeley was making his last major musical.* ☆

could out of this fragile project. Predictably, his prewar style of spectacular but empty-headed "girlie" numbers with little real dancing but lots of kaleidoscopic legs soon clashed with Gene's more realistic ideas about dancing being an extension of natural movement. When Berkeley would yell: "Take the camera back," meaning the shot should be wide enough to encompass an overall but old-fashioned view of the steps but with no real people, it was Gene who countered with: "Yeah, way back to 1929." In the end Berkeley left the set pleading exhaustion. Although he took sole director's credit for *Take Me Out to the Ball Game* (or, as it was known in baseball-ignorant Britain, *Everybody's Cheering*) he was never again to direct a major musical, leaving the field clear for Kelly and Donen, at first together and then separately, to fill the gap.

In later years Stanley Donen was to resent what he saw as unwarranted praise for Kelly at his own expense but during all the golden years, from their earliest days in Hollywood, Donen and Kelly were always a team, in public and in private. Stanley virtually lived with Gene and Betsy; he was there for all the Games and all the volley-ball tournaments. He married Jeanne Coyne, who was to become Kelly's second wife, and their lives were inextricably bound. Not noted for his

generosity to his colleagues, Kelly never failed to acknowledge and highlight Donen's contribution to his work. It began almost accidentally, one friend helping out another. "Stanley needed a job. I needed someone to count for the cameraman," Gene said, "someone who knew the steps and could explain what I was going to do so the shot was set up correctly." Donen, having been a Broadway dancer, knew how to do that. Their collaboration grew out of this mutual need and flourished until it was one of the most celebrated of partnerships—both in front of and behind the camera—in the history of musicals. Why Donen thought he lacked sufficient credit for his contribution to Gene Kelly's films remains a mystery.

Despite their generational differences Kelly admired Busby Berkeley enormously and was very grateful to him. "Buzz was probably the most remarkable talent the Hollywood musical ever had. More than anybody else, he showed what could be done with a movie camera, long before there was a zoom lens or a helicopter. He was the first to tear away the proscenium arch for the movie musical ... in the space of about five years he did everything with a camera that can be done and he taught me always to look for new ways of doing things."

There was one more legacy that Buzz was to leave Gene. While casting the baseball players for this otherwise unremarkable musical he alighted on an eccentric comedian called Jules Munshin and cast him in only his second film. It was therefore here, rather than in the forthcoming *On the Town*, that the trio of Kelly, Sinatra and Munshin was born.

ABOVE *Frank Sinatra, Jules Munshin and Gene rehearse a musical number with Stanley Donen.* ☆

The 1945 Anchors Aweigh *was the first of Gene's three major collaborations with Frank Sinatra.* ☆

In An American in Paris,
*Gene played a former
GI turned painter who
falls for the waif-like
Leslie Caron.* ☆

Among the many highlights of Singin' in the Rain *was the Broadway ballet Gene performed with a vampish Cyd Charisse.* ☆

ABOVE *The third ballet sequence of* Invitation to the Dance *had Gene dancing with animated figures to Rimsky-Korsakov's* Scheherazade. ☆

LEFT What a Way to Go: *Gene Kelly and Shirley MacLaine in a 1964 all-star flop which might have done better as a musical—the book was by Gorder and Green and score by Jule Styne.* ☆

RIGHT *Putting Barbra Streisand through her paces on the unhappy set of* Hello, Dolly! ☆

OVERLEAF *In contrasting his own style with Astaire's, Gene observed that whatever he wore himself, he always looked like truck driver. This became less true with the passing years. Inset: With the honorary Oscar he was awarded in 1951.* ☆

9. Three Sailors in Manhattan, One American in Paris

If *Take Me Out to the Ball Game* was an extremely creaky tribute to the all-American male, Kelly's next project was to be vastly more exciting. It stands today alongside *Singin' in the Rain* and *An American in Paris* as one of the greatest

Hollywood musicals ever, and one of Kelly's three masterpieces. It had begun as a ballet in New York and was devised by a young dancer-choreographer called Jerome Robbins to complement music by a little-known composer who had

> *"In 1949 the idea of dancing and singing in the streets of New York, using the city as a set, was revolutionary and certainly paved the way for 'West Side Story'. It was after 'On the Town' that musicals opened up."*
>
> GENE KELLY

recently scored a tremendous success by taking over from Bruno Walter at short notice to conduct the New York Philharmonic. The composer was Leonard Bernstein, the ballet was *Fancy Free*.

RIGHT *With Frank Sinatra and co-director Stanley Donen, Gene rehearses a rooftop number for* On the Town, *the story of three sailors on leave in Manhattan.* ☆

It was a bittersweet romp about three young sailors in wartime on a twenty-four-hour leave in Manhattan. Two of them meet girls, while the third sees a photograph of a girl in the subway, then persuades his friends to help him find her. The ballet was an immediate hit and has never been out of the repertoire of American Ballet Theater in the intervening fifty years. Bernstein's friends, the young revue artists Betty Comden and Adolph Green, wrote some lyrics to the ballet's episodes—largely—for fun, and they all suddenly realized what they had. As *On the Town*, it opened on Broadway with a cast which included Comden and Green, and the little group of New York bohemians who were scratching to make ends meet in Greenwich Village woke up the following morning with a massive mainstream hit. It was immediately bought for Hollywood by MGM, which promptly and characteristically shelved it, having decided to put Kelly and Sinatra into *Anchors Aweigh* instead.

Five long years later, with the war over and the sailors all home, Kelly had the clout to insist on making the picture the way he wanted. He co-directed with Stanley Donen, and the experience he had brought home from the Brooklyn Naval Yard after the war was triumphantly applied to produce an innovative movie. Kelly always said that *On the Town* was remarkable for being the first musical to be shot on location on the streets of New York in the actual places named in the plot. However, before we get too carried away by Gene's claims that this was an all-location picture, it needs to be recalled that on a low budget of $1,500,000 and a forty-six-day shooting schedule, they were only allowed five days on the streets of New York and for two of those days the rain was so heavy that shooting proved impossible. So what *is* truly remarkable is that in three days they managed an almost infinite number of "set-ups," some quite complex dancing and several songs. Working on the streets, they couldn't use either policemen to hold back the crowds or technicians to play back the music. So Kelly and Sinatra and the rest of the cast danced and sang to the beat of a small metronome in Kelly's pocket. If you look carefully in the exterior scenes you can catch glimpses of large numbers of passers-by watching the filming.

Lennie Hayton was again the musical director, and Roger Edens, who was working on the film as associate producer to Arthur Freed, is credited with writing additional music to supplement the Bernstein-Comden/Green score. To make it more commercial for the film version they dropped one of Bernstein's most beautiful ballads, "Lonely Town," which has only recently been

LEFT On the Town *was the first musical to include (albeit brief) scenes shot on location in the streets of New York. Sinatra, Munshin and Kelly drew fascinated crowds.* ☆

rediscovered. But Edens was a realist and he knew Mayer wasn't really behind the film. As he said later: "But for Freed this one would never have happened. He turned us loose on it, allowed us a revolutionary five-week rehearsal period, and by the time we got in front of the cameras we could have shot the whole picture backwards, we knew it so well."

The result was one of the most joyous and lyrical celebrations of the wonderful town itself, the American can-do excitement of the immediate postwar period, and the sheer exuberance of its youthful optimism. No film could better have launched Hollywood into the 1950s, the last great decade of the screen musical. On its first release it took more than $4,500,000, more than three times its budget; and if imitation is indeed the sincerest form of flattery then within the next five years Hollywood was to flatter *On the Town* with *Skirts Ahoy*, *All Ashore*, *Three Sailors and a Girl*, *So This is Paris*, and with Gene's next contribution to the genre, *It's Always Fair Weather*.

But what most matters about *On the Town* is its perfect example of musical flow; everything in it advances the plot, there are no extraneous cues for songs and no irrelevant balletic interpolations. There are no implausible backstage stories or daft fantasies; Kelly's courage meant that we could follow him anywhere down familiar streets and into a dance.

Even so, the early previews were not good as Gene himself recalled: "The film was very daring for its time and L.B. Mayer hated the fact that we had used blacks and Japanese-Americans in major roles as well as throwing out the chorus. When Stanley and I built our team at MGM we were an angry young group because up to that time musicals had been despised. Every good director would say 'One day I'll have some fun and make a musical,' and those films went right into the bucket. To make a musical in which people don't just say 'I love you' and then burst into song was real hard work, but we did it. And once I had broken the ice, and *On the Town* had become a hit, Metro let me do pretty much what I liked."

Amazingly, Gene was not nominated for an Oscar and neither was Sinatra. In fact, *On the Town* was only nominated in the musical scoring category and Roger Edens and Lennie Hayton took home the statues. Gene was in fact never to win an Oscar for any of his films, despite several nominations. The only one he ever took home was a special one in 1952— "In appreciation of his versatility as an actor, singer, director and dancer and specifically for his brilliant achievement in the art of film choreography"—and, sadly, Kelly didn't even get to collect that one: he was filming in

RIGHT *The Black Hand gave Gene a rare and welcome opportunity to play a dramatic role as gang leader Johnny Columbo.* ☆

Europe at the time and received the news over a crackly long-distance telephone. However, in 1982 the President of the United States was to present him with the Kennedy Award for Achievement in the Arts, and in 1985 the American Film Institute gave him its Life Achievement Award.

By the end of the 1940s Gene's MGM contract was worth $2,500 a week but he was still never in the top ten box-office star ratings and was not entirely happy with Metro's refusal to cast him in major dramatic roles. Fortunately for him, however, just as the editing of *On the Town* was completed, an MGM contract star slightly higher up the roster, Robert Taylor, had to drop out of a low-budget Mafia thriller called *The Black Hand*. Kelly took over the role in an otherwise almost entirely Italian cast and, although shot in only three weeks, this gangland revenge melodrama was over the years to make more money than many of Metro's more spectacular ventures. For his part, Gene was so convincing as Johnny Columbo, leader of the Black Hand gang, that for several years afterwards journalists believed his origins were Italian rather than Irish.

His next picture took him back to Judy Garland for the first time since *The Pirate* two years earlier. But *Summer Stock* was to be a much less happy project. The story of a troupe of show people doing a musical in a barn had been conceived by the producer Joe Pasternak as yet another "Let's do the show right here" vehicle for Mickey Rooney and Judy. But as they were now ten years beyond their prime Pasternak realized he would have to update; his way of doing so was simply to offer the Rooney role to Gene. After the trail-blazing *On the Town* Gene was less than happy about this already-dated idea but his devotion to Garland, who had just lost *Annie Get Your Gun* to Betty Hutton and was in real trouble with her studio contract, overcame his reluctance. His misgivings proved justified, as he later explained: "We had to babysit her all through the film; I would take her left arm and the director Charles Walters would take her right and between us we literally tried to keep her on her feet. There were times when we had to nail down supports so she wouldn't fall over and the whole experience was a ghastly, hideous nightmare which happily is a blur in my memory. I think we all knew this was a piece of crap but every day that Judy failed to appear on the set I at least managed to get a basketball championship going in the rehearsal room. All of us wanted to cut our losses and abandon the picture but Mayer took the unusually generous view that if we did so it would be the end of Judy and so we had to carry on to the bitter end."

And bitter it was: ten years behind its time, *Summer Stock* signally failed to transcend its material and repeat the success of *For Me and My Gal* or *The Pirate*, whatever it did for Gene's basketball skills. This was to be Judy's last MGM movie and she would not make another film until *A Star is Born* five years later. But everybody on the set noted Gene's generosity in the face of her increasingly impossible behavior. Gene himself said: "I loved her, understood what she was going through, and had every reason to be grateful for all the help she had given me in better times." June Allysen was the original casting for Judy's role, and thought a bit less likely to cause trouble on the set than Garland, it was generally thought she had been lucky to escape a disappointing script and derivative movie.

One night in the late 1940s Arthur Freed and Ira Gershwin happened to be together at a concert devoted to the music of Ira's brother, George, which included his *An American in Paris Suite*. As they talked in the interval, Freed told Ira that it had long been his dream to make a musical in Paris and asked whether Ira, as a representative of the Gershwin estate, would sell him the title. Ira agreed on one condition: that all the music in the film should be George Gershwin's. This was clearly to be a "class" project. Alan J. Lerner was hired to write the script, Johnny Green and Saul

Chaplin were brought in as musical directors, and Vincente Minnelli was to direct. The only problem was to decide whether Fred Astaire or Gene Kelly should play the ex-GI artist of the title. With *On the Town* by now a runaway success and Fred already in a kind of semi-retirement it didn't take them long to settle on Kelly. But the rest of the casting proved rather more difficult. As so often in Kelly's musicals the storyline, even though here by Lerner, was very slight. Gene, as the ex-GI staying on in Paris after the war to study painting, makes friends with an American concert pianist (Oscar Levant, Gershwin's great friend and interpreter, to lend a little authenticity) and falls in love with a beautiful young nightclub singer, before winning her heart in one of the most ambitious of all screen finales: the ballet to the entirely rescored *An American in Paris Suite*.

When Maurice Chevalier turned out to be unavailable, Georges Guetary, in his only American film, stepped in to play Gene's rival in love. But the real casting dilemma was where to find the seventeen-year-old French ingénue on whom the whole film turns. Leslie Caron's foreword to this book tells the story of how she came to be chosen for the role that was to make her as much of a star as *Roman Holiday*, another classic location picture of this time, had made of Audrey Hepburn. From

LEFT *With Judy Garland on the set of* Summer Stock. *The stale material and her deepening problems made this third collaboration an unhappy experience.* ☆

then on the two actresses were frequently to be suggested for the same roles: it was Leslie who got to film *Gigi*, in the role created on stage by Audrey, and it was Audrey who got to do the other great Parisian musical of the 1950s, *Funny Face*. The resemblances didn't stop there. They were both dancers—Leslie headed for a ballet career, Audrey eking out a living in nightclubs—and the tiny, waif-like figures of both young women were belied by their huge eyes and photogenic cheekbones. Once they got to see them, the cameras loved them.

Because the central character was a painter, *An American in Paris* is heavily influenced by Impressionism: the Paris Opéra is seen through the eyes of Van Gogh, even though he never painted it; Dufy is the inspiration for the ballet in the Place de la Concorde; and Renoir and Utrillo inspire many of the other street scenes.

The MGM hierarchy, now led by Dore Schary after the unceremonious and unlamented ousting of Louis B. Mayer, viewed the project with their usual caution and alarm. When Gene came up with his plan to end the film with the ballet he was, naturally, told it couldn't be done. As he recalled: "The first time you tried to do anything new at MGM you were in trouble. Even Irving Berlin took the time to come over and tell me that filming seventeen minutes of ballet with no words

simply couldn't be done. In fact, I knew it already had been; two years earlier the British film-makers Michael Powell and Emeric Pressburger had made *The Red Shoes*, in which Moira Shearer, Robert Helpmann and Leonide Massine did an exactly seventeen-minute ballet. Not only did nobody complain, the film made money all over America." Gene eventually won, but there's always a price for everything. In this case it had to do with his choice of location.

"MGM were prepared to let us shoot in Paris. But after all the arguments the city council wouldn't allow it. Metro, who never liked to admit they'd been thwarted, simply put it out that they preferred to shoot it on a backlot because 'Kelly couldn't dance on cobblestones.' Believe me, I've danced on a lot worse. In the event, all we had were two establishing shots of Paris."

The highlights of the picture included not just the ballet, filmed in seven weeks after the rest of the picture was in the can at an unbelievable cost for the time of $500,000, but also a number of other unforgettable sequences. Wedded to Gershwin's already-familiar score, Gene had to find new ways to present songs that had been used on the screen before. How, he wondered, could "I Got Rhythm" be made fresh again? The solution was typically simple and effective. He would

ABOVE *A relaxed moment with director Vincente Minnelli and co-star Leslie Caron during the shooting of* An American in Paris. ☆

teach that most American of songs to a group of little French children and show them how to dance in the process. The other great set-piece number, "Our Love is Here to Stay," takes place on the banks of the Seine. The seventeen-year-old ballet student, Leslie Caron, like Gene classically trained, was able to make the very difficult modern ballet choreography look like an extension of walking. Set in a circle within sight of a backlot version of Notre Dame, the dance builds from a walk to social dancing, to the sung duet, then to the more complex ballet, ending in a simple walk away from the camera.

Officially the director was Minnelli but so strong was Gene's control over the film that Vincente was able to take long leaves of absence even during the shooting—first a month to direct another picture altogether, and then several extra days to sort out the final complications of his agonizing split from Judy Garland. Nonetheless, several of the film's best ideas were his: it was he who thought of bringing in Preston Ames, an artist who had studied in Paris during the 1920s, to decorate the set; it was he who thought of the Artists' Ball being all in black and white (a device shamelessly lifted six years later by Cecil Beaton for the "Ascot Gavotte" sequence of *My Fair Lady*). Gene's two longtime assistants, Jeanne Coyne and Carol Haney,

RIGHT An American in Paris *turned Leslie Caron, the seventeen-year-old ballet dancer discovered by Gene, into a major star.* ☆

took on much of the choreography but it was of course the megalomanic Oscar Levant who had the idea of playing the Gershwin *Concerto in F* as every single member of the orchestra.

The film therefore was an amalgam of the best ideas by the best in the business. Even so, there was the usual doubt about how it would play in Peoria. Or Paris, for that matter. French critics immediately acclaimed it as the greatest movie musical ever made, but the review that mattered was Bosley Crowther's in the *New York Times*: "Count a betwitching French lassie by the name of Leslie Caron and a whoop-de-doo ballet, one of the finest ever put on screen, as the most commendable enchantments of *An American in Paris*, which is spangled with pleasant little patches of amusements and George Gershwin's tunes. It also is blessed with Gene Kelly, dancing and singing his way through minor romantic complications in the usual gaudy Hollywood gay Paree. But it is the wondrously youthful Miss Caron and that grandly pictorial ballet which placed the mark of distinction on this lush Technicolor escapade."

An American in Paris won Oscars for Best Picture, Best Cinematography, Best Screenplay, Best Art Direction, Best Musical Direction and Best Costumes. But neither Gene nor Leslie Caron received acting honors, nor yet Vincente Minnelli for his co-direction.

LEFT *The all-Gershwin score, unforgettable dance sequences and the ballet finale make* An American in Paris *one of the greatest of all film musicals.* ☆

RIGHT *An American in love. A deliriously happy Gene sings "S'Wonderful."* ☆

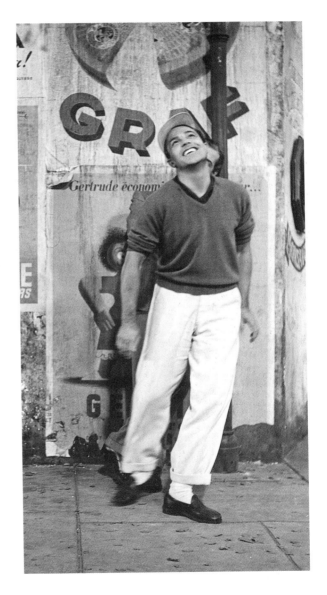

10. Let the Stormy Clouds Chase Everyone from the Place

No sooner was *An American in Paris* in the can than MGM urged Gene to join yet another of its all-star Singathons. This one, *It's a Big Country*, was a ludicrous compendium of eight short stories intended to celebrate "The Greatest Country in the World" at precisely the moment when a terror of Communism and the coming war in Korea was making the USA distinctly paranoid. Kelly was cast as a breezy young Greek called Icarus Xenophon falling in love across ethnic boundaries with the daughter of a Hungarian shopkeeper. Romeo and Juliet it wasn't; instead, the heavily underlined moral was that true love can overcome differences in the greatest of all melting-pot nations. They are all, after all, Amurricans. By now, however, there was something very much better on Gene's horizon: arguably the last great film he would ever make and the third in the remarkable sequence that had begun with *On the Town* only two years earlier.

> "Quite simply, it is the most enjoyable of all movie musicals and just about the best of all time"
> PAULINE KEEL

RIGHT *The elderly title song was what least attracted Gene to* Singin' in the Rain, *but he made it his own in perhaps the most famous dance in all Hollywood history.* ☆

Arthur Freed, Gene's mentor at MGM and the head of its music division, had by now produced forty major musicals since 1939 and decided (since he was also, of course, a distinguished lyricist) that the time had come to celebrate his own words and music. What he had in mind was to use the cream of his work over a number of years, and he had already decided that it was to carry the title of the first great hit that he and Nacio Herb Brown, his composing colleague, had enjoyed way back in 1926.

The song had, in fact, already been used in MGM's second musical, the 1929 *Hollywood Review*, in which it was sung by Buster Keaton and Marion Davies. Freed saw no reason not to use it again, some twenty-two years later. Gene was less enthusiastic. He liked the idea that Comden and Green had given Freed as a structure for the film but hated the notion of using a song that had already had at least two airings. Betty Comden was typically practical: "You like the movie, Gene, get used to the title."

That title was, of course, "Singin' in the Rain" and although he did finally accept it Gene was still sulking when Freed asked him what kind of dance he was going to do to it. "What can I tell you?" he grumped. "It's going to be raining and I'm going to be singing." He added one line at the end of the song, which

was, predictably: "I'm singin' and dancing in the rain." Apart from that he performed the song exactly as Freed had written it.

When Comden and Green began to work on the screenplay, all they had in mind was a little sketch they had first performed at the Village Vanguard in New York and later at the Westport summer theater where they first met Gene. It concerned a celebrated silent-screen star having to cope with the coming of sound. Almost at once they realized that if this was to work on film, it would have to be vastly extended to encompass an entire history of Hollywood as it had been in 1927 when the revolution occurred. The central characters were to be Don Lockwood, a matinee idol of the silent screen (Gene) and Kathy Selden (Debbie Reynolds, then aged nineteen), a movie extra. Their romance is interrupted by the arrival of the talkies, a singularly vacuous co-star, Lina Lamont (Jean Hagen), and Gene's wise-cracking sidekick, Cosmo Brown (Donald O'Connor). Around this star quartet Comden and Green built a wonderfully satiric picture of Hollywood life, much like the one they would devise a year later about Broadway for Fred Astaire and Jack Buchanan (*The Bandwagon*).

Singin' in the Rain drew on a rich catalog of Freed and Brown songs, not least the tongue-twisting "Moses Supposes," the exuberant wall-dancing "Make 'Em Laugh" and, of course, Kelly splashing through the puddles for the title song, perhaps the most quoted and reshown of all his solo numbers. Later, Comden and Green were to report that in Paris both François Truffaut and Alain Resnais treated them as royalty in view of their association with Chantons sous la Pluie. Gene himself, although privately always more fond of *On the Town*, came to understand why the film was the audience favorite of all time. As he said: "This was the golden age of the Hollywood musical and it was all due to Arthur Freed. He knew talent and how to use it, what projects were best to do and which people were best to work on them. He was a nonpareil, and when I think back about all the people I had the good fortune to work with under his gentle command, I'm just amazed."

In *Singin' in the Rain* there are about seven dance routines of such breathtaking complexity that dancers the world over, from Mikhail Baryshnikov to Twyla Tharp, study them on video, often unable to reproduce them. As Jean Hagen rarely had to interact with any of the others and she neither sang nor danced, the musical numbers were produced in a self-contained unit consisting of Stanley Donen, a stripped-down technical crew, and the other three stars. Gene was

ABOVE *Gene's long collaboration with Stanley Donen was among the most successful and celebrated in the history of musicals, though in later years Donen felt that he had not received the credit that was due to him.* ☆

LEFT *Donald O'Connor, Stanley Donen and Gene Kelly pose together for a publicity shot.* ☆

fortunate in having a young and infinitely malleable Debbie Reynolds to teach in his style and the brilliantly versatile Donald O'Connor, borrowed from another studio and capable of any kind of athletic dancing Gene could invent. O'Connor was a remarkably quick study, able to retain even the most unusual of step combinations after seeing them only once. He was always the most easy-going of actors, not really a leading man, and thrilled to be working on a film with the best crew and production team in Hollywood.

Gene, while taking infinite pains to teach the others what he needed them to do, was actually a one-man performing band, relying far more on Stanley Donen's counting and shot placements than on others in the scene with him. A good example is the "Moses Supposes" number, where Gene and O'Connor, are dancing together. O'Connor rarely, if ever, takes his eyes off Kelly except when the choreography imposes a change of direction, but Gene doesn't look once at O'Connor during the entire number except when the choreography insists on it. He simply assumed that they would both be in the right place at the right time; if not, Stanley Donen would say so after the take. In his solo number, however, O'Connor manages the entire backbreaking dance in only four shots, an act of virtuoso dancing almost unequaled

BELOW *In an MGM*
rehearsal hall Gene and
the nineteen-year-old
Debbie Reynolds work
on a dance routine. ☆

even today. There is no question who was the
better dancer. But then, Gene never really
wanted to be a great dancer. "I never was
crazy about performing; even as a dancer I
liked to create the stuff, I liked directing, but
I never really worked at the dancing."

In a film for which only three of the
numbers were original, the recycling job
performed by Comden and Green was nothing
if not remarkable. The genius of their *Singin'*
in the Rain screenplay is that it is constantly
referential but never reverential. It doesn't
take a Hollywood historian to spot in the
character of the director more than a faint
echo of Busby Berkeley, while the studio boss
was quite clearly inspired by Freed himself,
and there is even a gossip columnist who is
meant to be Louella Parsons.

Cyd Charisse, dancing the Broadway ballet
in which Kelly looks like Fairbanks as
d'Artagnan, modeled her look on that of
Louise Brooks, while the Jean Hagen dumb
blonde was an obvious act of homage to the
Judy Holliday appearance in the original
sketch with The Revuers of the Village
Vanguard, on which Comden and Green had
based the screenplay. In the film which
the writers themselves described as "an
irrepressible ode to optimism," only Donald
O'Connor is playing a character not drawn
from some kind of Hollywood reality, although

here too his character owed much to his own memories of his vaudeville childhood.

But in the end the memory is of a genial and loving parody of Hollywood in transition, rather than anything sharper or more satirical ,and it is in the title song that we find the extraordinary exuberance of Kelly's greatest success. "Everyone thought that the title number would be real difficult," he said, "but in fact it was the easiest of all my major dances. The real work was done by the technicians who had to pipe two city blocks on the backlot with overhead sprays, and the poor cameraman who had to shoot through all that water. All I had to do was skip down a sidewalk, climb a lamppost, have a drainpipe cascade on my face and jump around in puddles."

And that, according to Gene, in a nutshell, was *Singin' in the Rain*. Well, not quite. The dance and the lip-synching had to be split-second accurate. Kelly had to hit mark after mark that he couldn't see on an underwater dance surface that was slippery and unsafe. He never missed one. And that, according to the millions of viewers who have made it one of the most popular films ever made, was *Singin' in the Rain* in a nutshell.

The trouble was that it also represented the end of Kelly's golden years. At the age of forty, after only a decade in Hollywood, with forty-three years yet to live and twenty-four films still to make, the Kelly career was starting on its downward slope. *Singin' in the Rain* was an obituary for himself as well as silent Hollywood.

ABOVE *Reynolds, Kelly and O'Connor studying an old movie program. Their film was an affectionate parody of an earlier Hollywood era.* ☆

RIGHT *Gene centre stage in one of the big production numbers of* Singin' in the Rain, *described by its writers as "an irrepressible ode to optimism."* ☆

11. European Exile and an Undelivered Invitation

In December 1951, with *Singin' in the Rain* already being acclaimed at sneak previews as certainly the best musical since *The Wizard of Oz* a decade earlier, Gene took a decision which, on the face of it, meant professional suicide. The United States Congress had just passed a law offering a considerable tax break to any American who lived out of the country for more than eighteen months; in brief, they would no longer have to account to the Internal Revenue for any overseas earnings. This was, of course, the passport for countless MGM and other producers to start shooting their epics in Rome and London; but although it made very good sense for movie-makers in search of cheap extras, it made very little sense for an aging dancer who depended crucially on the Hollywood studio technology of the time.

> "By now, we simply had the wrong picture at the wrong time; by the late 1950s movie musicals had more or less died in America as in Europe"
>
> GENE KELLY

RIGHT *The most ambitious project of Gene's European exile, and perhaps of his career, was* Invitation to the Dance, *which he directed himself.* ☆

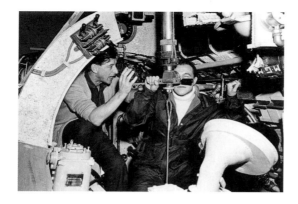

Nevertheless, Gene was almost the first star to announce his intention to live abroad for the full eighteen months, and although until now it has always been said by his chroniclers that the reason for his departure was purely financial there is perhaps an altogether different explanation. The House Un-American Activities Committee, semi-dormant since Gene's first brush with it in 1947, had now, under the renegade Senator Joseph McCarthy, burst back into horrendous activity. Careers were being destroyed all over town, victims were being forced into exile and, on at least two occasions, into suicide. Gene himself had nothing to fear from any of this: his leanings were always well known and libertarian rather than doctrinaire. His wife Betsy, however, never made any secret of her more radical views, and her support for a number of left-wing—indeed, early Communist—committees was widely known. Gene may well have thought that the family would not only be richer in Europe but also a great deal safer.

Accordingly, he convinced MGM that they should find him at least two European movies to keep him out of the country for the requisite length of time. Unfortunately, neither was even faintly distinguished and, as a result, Gene was to find himself, at the very moment when *Singin' in the Rain* was about to crown

his career, in a couple of low-budget programers made for the sole purpose of unfreezing Metro earnings abroad—unless of course you take the more sinister view that MGM was also punishing him for his decision to quit California. His relationship with the moguls, never close or friendly since David O. Selznick, had always been a purely professional one. He was often troublesome, an artist with decided views on how the films in which he was cast should be made. He cost them money by insisting on expensive experiments with mice and dustbin lids and "alter egos," and was never able to persuade rather than threaten. Directors (apart from the best of them, such as Minnelli) frequently found him overbearing and all too willing to encroach on their territory, and there had always been resentful complaints to studio chiefs about him.

Additionally, there was the problem of the Hollywood musical itself. In a long life of eighty-three years Gene only really had ten in which to establish his individual screen style. Amazingly, by the time he left Hollywood in 1950, the big musical revival to which he had so brilliantly contributed was, for economic reasons far beyond his control, already going into freefall. Many major musicals were made before the genre really collapsed in the 1960s but few showed any real sign of further

ABOVE *Gene in the British-made* Crest of the Wave, *which he said "was torpedoed and sank with all hands."* ☆

development. Most of the big-screen musical hits from now on would revert to photographs of the original Broadway stage shows.

The first of Gene's films in exile was *The Devil Makes Three*, a low-budget drama about an American army captain going back to Munich to find a family who had given him shelter during the war. In the process he gets caught up in a black-market racket involving a few surviving Nazi supporters. His co-stars were Richard Egan and the young Pier Angeli but there was little any of them could do to develop characterization for a director, Andrew Marton, who was best known for the chariot race in *Ben Hur* and still very keen on action over acting. Gene's verdict on the film was succinct: "a catastrophe," made even worse by the terrible irony that it was while in the middle of shooting it that Gene heard over the transatlantic telephone that not only had he won his special Oscar but there had been seven others that year for *An American in Paris*, including the award for Best Picture against such tough competition as *Quo Vadis*, *A Place in the Sun*, and *A Streetcar Named Desire*.

His second European picture was no better than the first, despite the fact that it was based on one of the longest-running of all Shaftesbury Avenue farces. This was *Seagulls Over Sorrento*, the story of a group of servicemen isolated on an island off the mainland of Scapa Flow. A London cast, led by Ronald Shiner and John Gregson, got five years out of this in the West End but by the time Gene began to film it for the Boulting Brothers (under the new title *Crest of the Wave*) it had already died a twelve-night death on Broadway—which should perhaps have been warning enough to MGM. However, they went ahead with the filming (Gene was the only American in an all-British cast) and when the movie finally arrived back at MGM in Hollywood all that Upstairs asked was could it please be given subtitles? Gene, maintaining the naval tradition of the picture, merely noted that: "It was torpedoed and sank with all hands."

Always conscious of his career path and of his aging dancer's body, Kelly was only too well aware that his future could hardly lie in low-budget B-movies shot in exile. He asked Carol Haney and Jeanne Coyne, his two trusted assistant choreographers, to join him in France because, between his two European disasters, he had started work on something he had always wanted to do and which only the huge success of *An American in Paris* and *Singin' in the Rain* could persuade MGM to allow.

It was now the summer of 1952 and Gene and the family had taken to the European life.

They first rented a villa outside Paris, where Betsy found work as a dialog coach on many of the American films that had been relocated in Europe to take advantage of the new tax breaks. After a while they also started to commute to London, where Gene kept a permanent suite at the Savoy and where he had enrolled their daughter, Kerry, now eleven, at the Royal Ballet School.

He needed assistance in the formulation of a full-length ballet film, the first of its kind ever conceived as a mainstream Hollywood production. *Invitation to the Dance* was hugely ambitious; even the budget of $600,000 did not truly reflect its revolutionary importance. Kelly's idea was that the film should consist of four separate ballets, each using the greatest dancers in Europe and America, thereby introducing them to audiences all over the world who had never been near a theater.

These four ballets were totally different in character. *Circus* was to be a semi-classical tragedy about a lovesick Pierrot falling to his death from the highwire while trying to impress the girl he loves. *Ring Around the Rosy* told a "La Ronde" story about a bracelet passing through a dozen different hands. Two of Britain's brightest young dance talents, Irving Davies and Paddy Stone, were to star alongside Tamara Toumanova and the New York City Ballet soloists Tommy Rawl and Diane Adams. In the third ballet (never filmed), Gene himself was to appear with all the dancers, in interpretations of a dozen songs from the American hit parade. The finale was to be a version of *Sinbad the Sailor* using a mixture of live action and animation, with Carol Haney dancing *Scheherazade* to the score by Rimsky-Korsakov. The idea was already over-ambitious and back at MGM headquarters in Hollywood Arthur Freed told Gene that he would have to cut the hit-parade ballet and promise to appear himself in the other three if the film was to have a hope of recouping its money. In fact it never did, and during the four years that it took *Invitation to the Dance* to reach American screens, almost everything that could go wrong with it surely did.

Even the score proved a nightmare. For the *Ring Around the Rosy* sequence Malcolm Arnold's original music was thrown out in rehearsal, but by the time André Previn was assigned the rewrite he had no idea at all what he was supposed to be doing. "I was presented," he later recalled, "with thirty minutes of silent film, some of which had originally been shot to Malcolm Arnold, some of it to Carol Haney just counting beats off camera, and most of it to nothing at all. Carol and I sat in a claustrophobic little music-department viewing theater for a month every day from 8 a.m. to midnight while she tried to remember the tempi and Gene's original ideas while I tried to chart some sort of musical framework. I have always hated jigsaws and this whole thing was a nightmare."

They finally put the picture together, not, as Gene had conceived it, as a brand-new but family-based happy show, but as a catalog of disasters—none of which he could have foreseen but all of which perhaps a Freed or a Minnelli might have prepared for. It ended up containing some innovative and often stunning dancing but, finally, it never cohered either filmically or choreographically.

The first sequence, with Gene as the tragic clown, was reckoned pretentious, while the second suffered not only from the problems that Previn has outlined but also because it was based on a Schnitzler original of which nobody back at MGM had ever heard. Therefore when Freed saw these first two sections his immediate reaction was to have the entire picture moved back to California and to throw another few thousand dollars at it, hoping that at least the last sequence could be made to stand up for American audiences.

This was *Sinbad the Sailor*, which then tied up Metro's animation department under William Hanna and Joe Barbera, plus Fred Quimby and forty other artists, for more than

a year. If the MGM brass had thought they were getting rid of their troubles with Kelly when he shipped off to Europe they were forced to think again. *Sinbad* required 250,000 drawings and 57,000 painted film frames from the animation cells to synchronize the cartoon characters with the live dancers. It was to be forty years before Disney, with animations such as *Beauty and the Beast* and *Aladdin*, would attempt anything on this scale. Once more, Gene was way ahead of his time.

Sadly, *Invitation to the Dance* fared so badly in its initial previews that Metro kept it on the shelf for another whole year and, as Kelly later explained, the delay proved disastrous. "When I originally set out to do the film, more than four years earlier, one of my chief reasons was the total lack of filmed dance material available to the general public.

"But by 1956 the situation had totally changed: people were seeing elaborate dancing on television variety shows and there was simply no need for our film. I also have to admit that there were some things in it that didn't come off as well as I had hoped and in the end I found myself agreeing with those who found the whole thing a bit much. Each ballet is enjoyable by itself but three in a row was probably more than most people could take at one cinema sitting."

RIGHT *The first sequence of* Invitation to the Dance *was "Circus," in which Gene played the tragic clown Pierrot.* ☆

12. For I Could Swim Loch Lomond and Be Home in Half an Hour

Gene's return to Hollywood early in 1954 was in dark contrast to his first arrival there fourteen years earlier. With Louis B. Mayer gone, Dore Schary was running a very different outfit at MGM, cutting costs and corners whenever and wherever possible. In Gene's European absence television had grown into a real threat; cinema attendance was nose-diving and Gene himself, with two European flops and *Invitation to the Dance* still in expensive post-production, was far from being flavour of the month. This was rapidly made clear to him when he suggested that for his next intended musical, *Brigadoon*, he and Minnelli should shoot on real Highland heather. Schary not only insisted on the whole thing being shot in California for budgetary reasons, but also demanded that they shoot in the new widescreen wonder, CinemaScope. "The studio betrayed us," complained a still-bitter Gene many years later. "It promised that all its picture houses were changing to CinemaScope, so we filled in the whole screen. Then we found that most movie houses were still showing in the old dimensions and most of the choreography was really messed up."

> "The way I look at a musical, you are commenting on the human condition no matter what you do. A musical may be light and frivolous, but by its very nature it makes some kind of social comment"
>
> GENE KELLY

RIGHT *For the Scottish fairy-tale musical* Brigadoon, *Gene was back in Hollywood and once again working with Vincente Minnelli, seen here with Jeannie Coyne who would later become Gene's second wife.* ☆

Brigadoon had been the first great Broadway hit for the team of Alan J. Lerner and Frederick Loewe in 1947. Among the score's many highlights was the now-classic "Almost Like Being in Love." It ran for more than 600 performances on Broadway and a further 700 in London, and won a Tony for Agnes de Mille's revolutionary choreography, which wedded classical ballet to traditional Scottish dancing and moved the story on within its own choreographic language. The story tells of two hard-bitten Manhattan businessmen who stumble upon a magic Scottish village that only materializes for one day every hundred years. One of them falls in love with a village girl and opts to remain in the village. The tale had been around for a while and owed a considerable if unacknowledged debt to J.M. Barrie, the Scots dramatist who frequently wrote of magical happenings north of the border.

But for the filming they weren't even north of Los Angeles. "We had researched shooting *Brigadoon* in Scotland," Gene said, "but it was too expensive to bring everybody there so we wanted to do in Northern California around the Highland Inn, which looked like it. My dream was to make a kind of Scottish Western, out of doors, but the studio said it couldn't afford that either, so we made it on a backlot as usual."

Brigadoon was to be the last time that Gene worked for the director Vincente Minnelli, who remembered it as a rather melancholy time: "We did the very best we could on the wrong locations; exteriors were enveloped with romantic mist and the interiors were lit to suggest Flemish paintings. Cyd Charisse made a lovely Scottish lass and we were helped immeasurably by Gene's usual assistants, Carol Haney and Jeanne Coyne. But this was to be Carol's last picture before she became a Broadway star in *The Pajama Game* and by now something was definitely missing. Gene seemed to have lost all faith in the project; he seemed curiously remote and slightly down. He had come back from Europe to find the musical genre at MGM in a steep descent. I had many talks with him, trying to impress on him the need to show exuberance in the part. If the film was to work, he had to light up the sky with his amazement at the miracle of Brigadoon. Gene just delivered as much as he could." In the end, it wasn't quite enough.

Gene had totally abandoned the original choreography to replace it with his own, designed, as he said, for the wide screen rather than the stage—feeling, as usual, that the cinema medium needed his understanding of the camera's movements. On Broadway, while every element of the show was praised (except

RIGHT *Cyd Charisse made a bonny Scots lass, but Gene and Minnelli knew they should have been shooting in Scotland.* ☆

for its "operettaish" plot), nearly all the critics had concurred with *Life* magazine when it declared: "*Brigadoon*'s real brilliance lies in its Scottish dances directed by Agnes de Mille." When the story faltered, it was generally agreed, the dances revived it. But Lerner and Loewe had clashed with de Mille and she, typically, found their clashes childish. The three of them were not a dream team and the great songwriters, not surprisingly, minimized her contribution to their show so they were relieved that Gene didn't want her to work with him on the film.

But the lyricist Lerner was also quick to realize the trouble they were in: "*Brigadoon* was a picture that should have been made on location in Scotland but was in fact largely done in the studio. It was a singing show that tried to become a dancing show and it had an all-American cast that should have been all-Scottish. It was one of those ventures that occur so often where we all know we are going down the wrong road but no one can stop. I have always believed that only genuinely talented people can create something that is genuinely bad. Only the mediocre are always at their best." As usual, Lerner was nearly right. As the lyricist he can be forgiven for ignoring the success of the dancing at the expense of the singing, but as to his overall point, it is undeniable that the film of

Brigadoon ended up as a kind of pudding instead of the soufflé it should have been.

When it opened, in the autumn of 1954, lovers of the original stage show were horrified to find that not only was the great de Mille sword dance missing but two of the best numbers ("Come to Me, Bend to Me" and "There but for You Go I") had been dropped. Moreover, the dubbing of Cyd Charisse's voice by Carol Richards for the songs was less than perfect, and in the third leading role the usually amiable Van Johnson looked more and more uneasy as every musical number proceeded. Reviews were just about as terrible as the team expected. *Newsweek* noted: "Despite the resurgence of good films, Hollywood can still put its worst foot forward and does so in *Brigadoon*." For the *New York Times* Bosley Crowther found it: "Curiously flat and out of joint, rambling all over creation and seldom generating warmth or charm—pretty weak, synthetic Scotch." A country that, while not famous for its appreciation of irony, had always had a capacity to enjoy whimsy, nonetheless rejected this most whimsical of films for its execution rather than its content.

As Minnelli has suggested, Gene was now at about the lowest ebb of his career and indeed his life. His marriage to Betsy Blair, one of Hollywood's firmest, was beginning to

LEFT *Gene and Minnelli on the set of the ill-fated* Brigadoon. *"We all knew we were going down the wrong road," said lyricist Alan J. Lerner, "but no one could stop."* ☆

show signs of strain as Betsy, on the strength of a much-acclaimed starring role opposite Ernest Borgnine in *Marty*, had begun to lead an increasingly separate life. Back in Pittsburgh, Harriet and James Kelly had stuck together through poverty, alcoholism and the trials of bringing up five children during the Depression. It was one of Gene's deepest convictions that marriage is for ever and that no matter what his troubles with Betsy were, they were nothing that could not or should not be transcended.

As if trying to retrieve some kind of family life, Gene begged MGM to give a chance to his brother Fred, who had been running a dance academy in New Jersey, to appear with him in yet another all-star composer biography. This was *Deep in My Heart*, starring José Ferrer as a somewhat dour Sigmund Romberg and Helen Traubel in her first film role as his lifelong friend. It followed slavishly the pattern of such earlier composer biopics as *Words and Music* in that guest stars were wheeled in for individual musical numbers hung together on a dangerously slender storyline. Gene had the idea of inviting Fred to join him in "I Love to go Swimmin' with Wimmen." This was to be their only joint screen appearance and, indeed, Fred's only film. It ran for all of five minutes and was generally reckoned to be the best routine in an

otherwise dire hotch-potch. In Pittsburgh it had been Fred whom Harriet had pinpointed for fame, not Gene. And this was it, Fred's one brief, shining moment.

Gene, at forty-three, was all too aware that he had drastically to alter the shape of his career. The great days of the Arthur Freed unit at MGM were clearly over. Should he perhaps return to New York and see what Broadway had to offer? He was still settled in California and in a battle to save his marriage. Betsy was getting film roles and had no interest in leaving. Was there perhaps a future for him as a straight actor? In this area he had already suffered several blows. Elia Kazan came close to offering him the role of Biff in the first Broadway *Death of a Salesman* but in the end offered him a much inferior script, Tennessee Williams's *Casino Royale*. He was also tentatively offered the film of *Teahouse of the August Moon*, only to have the role snatched away at the last minute by Marlon Brando.

But now, in 1955, came the biggest disappointment of his entire career. Samuel Goldwyn was about to film *Guys and Dolls*, and if ever there was a role tailor-made for the man who had been Pal Joey it was surely Sky Masterson, the street-smart gambler brought to heel by the Salvation Army doll. Goldwyn was keen to have him, but in Gene's own words: "Although I was born to play Sky the

way Gable was born to play Rhett Butler, those new bastards at MGM refused to loan me out."

This was of course the third time that Metro's possessiveness had denied him a role he craved. First Pal Joey and then Cyrano. Now, taking all that into consideration as well as Metro's treatment of his beloved *Invitation to the Dance* and what seemed to be its perennial lack of confidence in him and the musicals he wanted to make, Gene decided the time had come to bid farewell to the studio where he had worked for the past sixteen years. Before that final parting, however, he made one last attempt to get back to the old magic.

The third of the trio of musicals directed by Gene and Stanley Donen and written by Betty Comden and Adolph Green was to be *It's Always Fair Weather*. And just to underline the nostalgic quality of the project, the concept was to bring together three wartime buddies after a break of ten years to see how they had survived the peace. In contemporary film parlance this was meant to be *On the Town II*, but the problems began at an early stage. Of the original trio of sailors on their twenty-four-hour leave in Manhattan, Frank Sinatra had become too important (and too difficult) to be in any team, and Jules Munshin was not reckoned by the studio to mean anything at the box office. Accordingly, Dan Dailey was put into Sinatra's slot while

ABOVE *Gene and Stanley Donen directing Michael Kidd (left) during the shooting of* It's Always Fair Weather, *the film that cost him his relationship with Donen.* ☆

RIGHT *The high point of* Deep in My Heart *was a routine in which Gene was joined by his brother Fred, who was making his screen debut.* ☆

Munshin's comic buddy role was taken on by the dancer-choreographer Michael Kidd, then in great studio favor for his work on *Seven Brides for Seven Brothers* and *The Bandwagon*.

The score, this time entirely by André Previn, was functional rather than magical; the love interest was supplied by Cyd Charisse and Dolores Gray. But only two numbers—the celebrated dustbin-lid dance and Gene's amazing roller-skate ballet, recalling for him his boyhood triumphs on the ice rink—really lived up to their famous choreographic predecessors. When he had danced with the mouse or the mop or the shop window he had entered previously unexplored territory. Now, with the advent of Agnes de Mille (perforce off-screen because her impact on the stage musical had been so strong that movie-makers were afraid to hire her for fear of tipping their films into ballet interpretations) and the younger upcoming choreographers such as Michael Kidd, Gene seemed, albeit somewhat unfairly, to be merely repeating himself.

It's Always Fair Weather opened early in 1956 to dejected reviews, most of which complained about the crude use of color and the insurmountable problems of dancing on a CinemaScope screen. Worst of all, for Gene, was the fact that this movie, far from reviving old hits and long-term partnerships, actually destroyed his relationship with his lifelong friend, Stanley Donen. Hollywood insiders and close friends speculated that professionally Donen now needed to strike out on his own (in the next two years he was to direct on his own *Funny Face, The Pajama Game, Indiscreet* and *Damn Yankees*) while privately he was becoming all too aware of the affection that his wife, Jeanne Coyne, had for Gene— although it took Kelly, still wrapped up in his own troubles and never the most sensitive of husbands or lovers, at least two more years to realize it. Jeanne had for many years been his faithful assistant choreographer, his dancing muse and his close friend. What he didn't know was that she was in love with him, a love she only declared when she was certain that both their marriages were at an end. Whatever the cause of the rift, the two men were never quite able to make it up, and ever since then Donen has retained a great but inchoate resentment toward Gene.

The final irony of *It's Always Fair Weather*, as with many other films of its era, is that it was a sustained and neurotic attack on what Hollywood now perceived as its greatest enemy—the coming of television. However, as the film is today only ever shown on television, the younger medium gets its revenge by clipping off the dancers' feet and shrinking Gene's carefully composed CinemaScope frames to fit its own format.

The critic Barry Norman saw the reception of the film as an omen: "In 1955 the box-office failure of *It's Always Fair Weather*, co-directed by Kelly and his frequent partner Stanley Donen, indicated that the public appetite for musicals was by no means insatiable, and two years later Kelly's *Invitation to the Dance* was widely regarded by the more sour critics as heralding the very death of the screen musical."

That same year also saw the release of *Love Me Tender*, the first Elvis Presley musical; in light of that, for Gene as for Arthur Freed and the whole of the musicals unit, it was all over.

RIGHT *Performing the famous dustbin-lid dance in* It's Always Fair Weather *with Michael Kidd (left) and Dan Dailey (right).* ☆

13. Blithe as the Air of Springtime, Swift as the Summer Grass

By the time *Invitation to the Dance* was grudgingly released by MGM, fully four years after Gene had started work on it, he was already in negotiation with the studio about his release. His contract still had two more years to run but the deal struck was that if he would give MGM two more pictures he would be allowed to set up in independent production. The first of these was to be *The Happy Road*. "I had been sitting around for months waiting for an assignment," he recalled. "I couldn't stand not working, so finally we agreed on a co-production deal for any property of my choice. Unfortunately, they also insisted on my playing the lead, which I really did not want to do because producing and directing and being the star is just too much—but at this point I was desperate to broaden my horizons." What Gene forgot to mention is that, in addition to producing, directing and starring in the movie, he also wrote the lyrics for the title song. The only advantage of *The Happy Road* was that it was set (and could be shot) all over France, a country where Gene increasingly felt at home since the French respect for his work was considerably higher than anything he had recently known at home or in Britain.

> "The career of Gene Kelly remains something of an enigma. Just as he had confirmed his place as one of the most important talents ever to work in film he went downhill so fast you hardly saw him go"
>
> DAVID SHIPMAN

RIGHT *Performing Cole Porter's "You're Just Too Too" with Kay Kendall in* Les Girls. ☆

However, *The Happy Road* proved a very bumpy one indeed. It was a low-budget tale of two runaway children joining forces to find their respective parents. Inevitably, the search brings the adults together and what Kelly was trying to do with this very slender Harry Kurnitz plot was to satirize gently differences in the French and American characters.

American audiences proved deeply uninterested, as did MGM, and the picture ended up as the second half of a double bill ignored even by most critics. The location shooting, which should have been a joy for Gene, turned out to be nothing of the kind. His father, James, died during the filming and Betsy, having just won her Best Actress Award for *Marty* at the Cannes Film Festival, had finally decided to go for a divorce. And the weather was terrible.

On April 3rd, 1957, in Las Vegas, the Kellys' fifteen-year marriage ended when Betsy was given an uncontested divorce on the then-usual grounds of mental cruelty. Gene gave her a settlement of $200,000 in lieu of alimony, and they were awarded joint custody of their daughter Kerry. Soon afterward Betsy moved to London, where she has lived ever since with her second husband, the distinguished film director Karel Reisz. For Gene it was a terrible failure, as significant as any professional disaster he had ever suffered.

LEFT *Had* Les Girls *not been a musical, director George Cukor and Gene might have been more on the same wavelength.* ☆

To his rescue, emotionally and now romantically, came Jeanne Coyne (always known as Jeannie to avoid confusion with Gene), who now moved into his Hollywood home on North Rodeo Drive. She had always been there for him and theirs was to be an intensely happy and calm partnership. She bore him two more children, Tim and Bridget, before her untimely death from leukemia in May 1973.

And there was another kind of rescue on the horizon. Dore Schary, the MGM chief who had never been Gene's greatest fan, was abruptly dismissed from the studio at the beginning of 1957 and replaced by the rather more gentle and Gene-friendly Benny Thau. Benny had a problem. He had just bought a Broadway hit comedy called *The Tunnel of Love*, and had already cast Doris Day and Richard Widmark in the leading roles, but somehow he had failed to find a director. Something made him think of Gene, and his desperation was such that he made him an offer he couldn't refuse. If Gene could make the film in black and white on one set in three weeks for less than $500,000, he could choose one more musical and maybe start a whole new career.

Gene, never one to refuse a challenge, brought the film in on time and budget and thereby opened up, albeit inadvertently, a whole new career for himself as a director of non-musicals. But he still had one MGM film left to make. This was his last major musical and it was shot in Europe under circumstances which were very different from those of all the others. With the Arthur Freed unit soon to be disbanded and Gene no longer on any terms with Stanley Donen, the movie was to be directed by George Cukor, with choreography by Jack Cole. Only Cole Porter's score suggested any link back to the golden years, and even Porter was also now at the end of his film-musical career.

On paper *Les Girls* looked as though it would be one final, glowing tribute to the genre that Gene had done so much to develop. Not only did it have Cukor and Porter, two of the great stylists of all time, it also had three enchanting female stars in Kay Kendall, Taina Elg, and Mitzi Gaynor. The problem was the John Patrick screenplay, a complex series of flashbacks in which each dancer told more or less the same story but from totally different perspectives as a court case for slander is gradually sorted out. Jack Cole was taken ill during the shooting, and although Gene and Jeanne took over several of the dance numbers they were never really happy with Cukor who, while amiable enough, was essentially only interested in the movie when they stopped singing and dancing and started to act. This

gave *Les Girls* a curiously stop-start quality
from which it never quite recovered. Until that
time Cukor hadn't really displayed much
interest in the musical form, although,
memorably, he went on to direct *My Fair
Lady*, albeit somewhat stagily.

On the plus side, Porter's score, though by
no means his best, did allow Gene to dance
with all three of the girls and for once it
looked as though the Cinemascope problems
had been cracked. Kelly also got to do a
bizarre parody of Marlon Brando in *The Wild
One* and Kay Kendall, neither a singer nor a
dancer, nevertheless managed a wonderful re-
run of the drunk scene she had first played in
Genevieve. This final Kelly musical was
chosen to be the Royal Command Performance
film in 1957, but the British reviews mostly
reflected polite disappointment that so many
stars could have got caught up in so slender a
project.

For the first time in more than sixteen
years, Gene was now a totally free agent. The
problem was that the musicals to which he
had dedicated his working life were simply
no longer being made, and even if they had
been, he was a little old, at forty-six, to star in
them. A dancer's body, even one as highly
conditioned as Gene's, wears out early and
often, as in Gene's case, the knees go first.
Although financially comfortable, Gene was

by no means the multi-millionaire he would have been today. He had always been a contract player, well-paid but not excessively so, and his ability to provide for his family, while not in question, was not unlimited. He had essentially two options—to direct or to act —but he decided to combine the two. He lived for almost forty more years but he was never again to star in a major hit, although he guest-starred in several minor ones and was to live long enough to catch the contemporary passion for nostalgia. As one of the last great stars of the golden years he would become king of the retrospective anthologies.

For now, however, he chose to go down the straight-acting route, and when Danny Kaye had to drop out of *Marjorie Morningstar*, the screen adaptation of Herman Wouk's bestselling novel about a young girl (Natalie Wood) on the brink of womanhood and stardom who falls in love with an older man, it was Gene who stepped in. Kelly's character, a singer, dancer, songwriter, and director working the Catskills summer circuit was, in his own words: "A talented, brilliant fellow, the kind everyone thinks will take Broadway by storm. But he lacks either the guts or the drive, the ability or the confidence to push himself to the top. I've known a lot of people like this. Those who succeed in this business are not necessarily those with the most talent but those with the most stamina and the most luck." Although he was Irish Catholic rather than Jewish, Gene recognized himself as Noel Airman. He had always thought, like Harriet, that it would be Fred who became the star. In the event, it was Gene who turned out to have not only the ability but the luck, the stamina, the guts, and the drive.

Reviews for *Marjorie Morningstar* were respectful rather than rave and, as so often, it was Gene himself who put his finger on the problem. "Wouk's novel is not only about showbusiness; it's about upper-class Jews and their problems of assimilation. Nowadays, instead of Natalie Wood and me, they would cast Barbra Streisand and Dustin Hoffman and the whole story would make a lot more sense."

In December 1957, with *Marjorie Morningstar* safely in the can and Gene beginning to find confidence in his new-found dual career of actor and director, he took the family on a skiing holiday to Zermatt in Switzerland. The family consisted of Gene's ex-wife and future wife, and Kerry, now a student of the International School in Geneva. One afternoon, on his way back to the hotel from the ski-slope, Gene fell on some slush and totally ripped the cartilage in one of his knees. "Since that accident," he said, "I have never really worked as well; this really was the end of serious dancing for me."

ABOVE *Gene on the set of* The Tunnel of Love, *which he directed, with Richard Widmark and Doris Day.* ☆

LEFT *Gene rehearsing with Sugar Ray Robinson for a TV special, 1958.* ☆

By a happy coincidence, there was yet another totally new opportunity on the horizon. Amazingly, Gene had not been back to Broadway in any on-stage capacity since *Pal Joey*, eighteen years earlier; suitably enough, it was Richard Rodgers, composer of *Joey*, who now wanted to bring him back. Not as a dancer or a choreographer or even as an actor. What Rodgers wanted Gene to do was direct *The Flower Drum Song*, which he and Oscar Hammerstein had just completed. Set in San Francisco's Chinatown, this was a charming if fragile addition to the Rodgers and Hammerstein collection and its undoubtedly racial and chauvinistic plot makes it the least revived of all their shows. Hammerstein, who in *South Pacific* had already enraged white supremacists with his anti-racist "You've Got to be Carefully Taught," considered Gene (whose liberal views on race were widely known) to be exceptionally well qualified to direct a story about the clash of cultures within the Asian community. Kelly also saw this as a wonderful opportunity to reassemble the old team. Carol Haney was to be the choreographer and she, Gene, and Jeanne immediately set off on a Far East casting trip which would only be repeated some thirty years later when Cameron Mackintosh had to find suitable cast members for *Miss Saigon*. They returned with

the leads and several supporting actors, all of whom were to make their Broadway debuts alongside the more experienced Larry Blyden, Juanita Hall, and Anita Ellis.

The Flower Drum Song was the only Broadway show that Gene ever directed and it ran for a respectable if not record-breaking 600 performances. As Gene recalled: "This wasn't one of the best Rodgers and Hammerstein shows and in rehearsal both Oscar and the book-writer, Joe Fields, were taken seriously ill, which didn't help us any. Nor did the fact that our star, Larry Blyden, was just getting his divorce from our choreographer, Carol Haney, and they had to work together as though nothing else was going on in their lives. The score was nowhere near *South Pacific* or *Oklahoma!* but it had warmth and a sweet sentimentality about it. I knew that as long as I crammed the production brimfull of every joke and gimmick in the book I could make it work, but this was always an audience show rather than anything for the critics." In the words of Richard Rodgers: "What we most needed on *The Flower Drum Song* was a professional who could spark it all off. In Gene Kelly we got a man who was not only experienced and professional to the very marrow of his bones, but hard-working and inspired as well. Without him we could have been in a lot of trouble."

RIGHT *In one of his 1959 television specials Gene was joined by the thirteen-year-old Liza Minnelli, whose mother Judy Garland had been perhaps his most ideal dancing partner.* ☆

With nothing much to do back in Hollywood, and no movie offers anywhere on the horizon, Gene stayed in New York after the opening of *The Flower Drum Song* to see if any other Broadway offers might come his way. They didn't but something equally promising did. Alistair Cooke, then host of NBC's arts series, *Omnibus*, suggested to Gene that he should do a whole hour-long show on the nature of dance. Gene predictably leaped at the offer and made his agenda clear even in the program's title. It was called *Dancing: A Man's Game* and in it Gene tried to establish that there was no need for the association with effeminacy that still conditioned the American public's view of ballet. "Any man," he said on the show, "who looks sissy while dancing is just a lousy dancer. A good dancer simply takes the physical movements of sport and exaggerates, extends, and distorts them in order to show what he wants to say more clearly and more strongly. There's no difference between a footballer warming up for a game and a modern dancer going through his paces."

Gene's triumph with this first major dance documentary led on immediately to two more specials, one of which was described by the *New York Times* as: "Blithe as the air of springtime, swift as the summer grass, a merry mélange of interview, song and hoofing." The

show was indeed, for its time, remarkably experimental. Gene even commissioned a poem from America's poet laureate, Carl Sandburg, as a dance accompaniment. The same show introduced to American audiences for the very first time a gangling thirteen-year-old Liza Minnelli. But, as has always been the case with arts television, that was more or less that. *Omnibus* went on to other matters and Gene was left to reflect that television would never really have room for any kind of regular modern dance series. Later, of course, with the introduction of public television, there was a huge outpouring of dance programmes. Only recently, with the withdrawal of most federal funds for the arts and television, has it reverted to the state which so distressed Kelly.

In the summer of 1959 he was invited to serve on the jury of the Cannes Film Festival and, while the family was staying in Europe for a vacation, he had a telephone call from Hollywood inviting him to play what would in fact prove to be his last major role. And in tremendously distinguished company.

Stanley Kramer was about to direct *Inherit the Wind*, the celebrated Broadway hit by Lawrence and Lee about the "Monkey Trial" of 1925 which effectively put Darwin's theory of evolution in the dock. Spencer Tracy and Frederic March were cast as the opposing lawyers, Clarence Darrow and William Jennings Bryan, while Kelly was to play the great journalist H.L. Mencken, who had made his name covering the trial for the *Baltimore Sun*. For Kelly this was both a thrilling and a terrifying project. He had simply never worked on stage or screen with talents as great as those on parade here. As he said later: "It was impossible to learn anything from either of them because whatever they did came deep down from some inner part of themselves, which, for an outsider like me, anxious to learn, was totally inaccessible. All you could do was watch the magic and be amazed, and all I really learned from them was that no matter what I did, I would never be as good as they were." These moments of introspection in Kelly are rare and worth treasuring. One of the few unanswered questions that still hangs over the Kelly career is how good he would have been as a straight actor had he not primarily been a dancer-choreographer. After all, Billy Wilder had wanted to cast him for the William Holden role in *Sunset Boulevard*. But it is only very occasionally that one catches a glimpse of just how good Kelly could be as an actor. In that sense, *Inherit the Wind* was his finest hour. It is a pity that it was also close to his final hour as a serious actor.

ABOVE *Gene and Jeannie on their return to Los Angeles after a quiet wedding in Nevada in August 1960.* ☆

RIGHT Inherit the Wind *memorably gave Gene a rare chance to show what he could do in a serious role, though he himself felt that co-star Spencer Tracy would always be in a different league.* ☆

14. Hello Dolly, Bye Bye Barbra

Despite its excellent ingredients, *Inherit the Wind* was not a box-office success and it led Kelly, as so often in these later years, precisely nowhere. Reluctantly, he went back to television for some routine specials. As Clive Hirschhorn notes: "Gene, the erstwhile innovator who had taken the movie musical by the scruff of its neck and shaken it free of cobwebs, seemed content now to spend his time appearing in lucrative television specials, more or less recapping his career in musicals for the benefit of a new American generation already too young to have remembered him in his heyday."

> *"Kelly's career was built as a performer but, given the specialized nature of dance, he was compelled to become first a choreographer and then a director in order to realize his ambition as a dancer. By the time he reached the summit of his career, his dancing days were already on the way out"*
>
> PETER WOLLEN

RIGHT *With Marilyn Monroe and Yves Montand during his one-day contribution to the musical* Let's Make Love, *in a guest role as Montand's dance teacher.* ☆

In the following year, however, something vastly more intriguing and challenging did come along.

The ballet company of the Paris Opéra, then trying to drag itself into the twentieth century, invited Kelly to create a modern ballet, building on his experiences in *Invitation to the Dance*. Once again, as for *An American in Paris*, he decided to use the music of George Gershwin, and to base the ballet (an eccentric bedroom farce about Aphrodite coming back to earth) on his *Concerto in F*.

Predictably, the ballet split Parisian audiences into those who approved of Kelly's innovations and those who would rather have had another *Swan Lake*. Yet again, it was a one-off. As usual, he was respected for his professionalism, admired for his ideas and applauded for his ability to wrest order from chaos. But he never became a member of anyone else's team, never would play for a scratch side, never really liked groups. So each separate experience was a success but also a dead end. Yet at least in Paris he was now getting all the honors he felt were denied him at home. *An American in Paris* and *On the Town* had already been acclaimed by French critics as the greatest musicals of all time; he was made a Knight of the Legion of Honor at a ceremony at the Opéra and, still more importantly to him, was presented by Jean

Cocteau with a Lifetime Achievement Award from the Cinémathèque Française, an honor given to only two other foreigners: Alfred Hitchcock and Fred Zinnemann.

Back home in Los Angeles, in August 1960, Gene finally decided to propose to Jeanne, much to the delight of Kerry who thought it should have happened years earlier. With a new family, Gene had to keep working. Accordingly, he next took a brief guest-starring role teaching millionaire Yves Montand to dance in a curiously disastrous Marilyn Monroe musical called *Let's Make Love*. His scene took exactly one day to shoot and the following morning he was on a plane to Paris to direct Jackie Gleason in *Gigot*. Admirable in concept and catastrophic in execution, this was Gleason's attempt to reposition himself from television sitcom villain to lovable Chaplinesque clown in a series of minor adventures written from his own outline. In the event Kelly could not save a fragmented script, and ninety-five minutes of Gleason virtually alone on screen being alternately lovable and winsome was enough to curdle the strongest stomach.

Only two good things happened during *Gigot*: two telephone calls from California. The first brought the news that Jeanne was pregnant with Timothy ("Your present is inside me," she wrote on a birthday card); the second call offered a twenty-six week series of television dramas based on the 1944 Bing Crosby hit, *Going My Way*. The series happily occupied the next six months of Gene's life while he was waiting to be a father again. But, scheduled against the triumphant *Beverly Hillbillies*, it never really stood a chance in the ratings and was quietly dropped at the end of the first series.

While his home life was now going from strength to domestic strength, his working life over the next two years was to be infinitely depressing. Project after project went down in flames around him. The first of these was an ambitious plan he devised with Frank Sinatra, whereby Gene would join Frank's Ratpack on a three-picture deal. Kelly was to produce the first, star in the second and direct the third, while Sinatra and Dean Martin starred in all three.

Sinatra, who often had nothing good to say about anybody, was always genuinely fond of Kelly. In a way, the poor Italian Catholic boy from Hoboken had found an echo in the poor Irish Catholic boy from Pittsburgh and somehow the admiration had stuck throughout both their star careers. Sinatra, always sensitive to real or imagined slights, found the often insensitive Gene admirable. "Gene's ... fierce urge for perfection, his almost fanatical need for success, have always

been matched by his need for justice for the less gifted, or less advantaged, whose paths crossed his. Gene climbed to the top but he didn't step on any hearts on the way up." But, typically, Gene couldn't get the Ratpack to give him any coherent start dates, and *Robin and the Seven Hoods* was eventually made with other hands.

Next of the major disappointments was a remake of *Beau Geste* for which the money could not be found; a third was a screen adaptation of the Broadway comedy, *Send Me No Flowers*, which Gene was to direct, but abandoned when the studio insisted on Bobby Darin over his preferred choice of Warren Beatty in the leading role. Ultimately, the picture limped on to the screen with Rock Hudson. Almost another year was to be wasted as Gene tried to set up a major English movie musical, one which never made it even as far as the rehearsal room.

It had been four years since *Inherit the Wind* had given Gene any kind of screen credibility and all he could do now, as money for movies dried up, was to wait for the phone to ring. He was a proud man, so this was humiliating—especially because when the phone did ring it seldom led to anything constructive.

His next film was again only fractionally better than a guest slot. 20th Century-Fox had

finally decided to go ahead with a film originally designed for Marilyn Monroe and inevitably shelved after her death in 1962. Over the previous two years it had been offered to both Elizabeth Taylor and Kim Novak but it was Shirley MacLaine who was finally lumbered with the role of the simple country girl who marries six millionaires, all of whom come to a sticky end, in what was now called *What a Way to Go*.

Gene therefore joined a lineup of Robert Mitchum, Bob Cummings, Dick van Dyke, Dean Martin and Paul Newman; but at least he got to play, albeit briefly, a nightclub hoofer trampled to death by his own fans. He choreographed the one number he shared with MacLaine to a score by Jule Styne; it was meant to be a lampoon of the worst of Busby Berkeley but as the film itself was worse even than that, the joke went unnoticed.

Domestically, his second marriage had radically changed Gene's Hollywood life. Jeanne had never cared for the social gatherings around the volleyball court or the endless Games of charades and, as she herself gave up working to have their son and daughter, it was as though a fence had gone up all around the property. From now on the Kellys dedicated themselves to parenting instead of socializing. Gene had always taken his role as father very seriously but whereas

with Kerry he was working flat out and often on location, with Tim and Bridget he was a hands-on parent, always there, always available. Neighbors, and fans who sought out the Rodeo Drive house as a tourist attraction, were often startled to see a famous movie star careering around the property on roller skates with his children in tow. Harriet and James Kelly had done their job.

Although he was therefore keen to stay home as much as possible, one offer intrigued Gene enough to take him back to France. The French director Jacques Demy had just had a huge hit with that rarity of all rarities, a post-war French film musical. He now wanted to follow his *Umbrellas of Cherbourg* with a companion piece, *The Young Girls of Rochefort*, and he was keen that Gene, who had always been his great idol, should come over to star in it. That also, of course, not entirely coincidentally, would mean he would have a reasonable chance of success at the American box office. But Gene, at fifty-five, was no longer on form. His voice had to be dubbed for the first and only time, and his dancing had to be limited to a couple of numbers. The plot was flimsy and not helped by the casting of two French stars, Catherine Deneuve and Françoise Dorléac (sisters in real life), neither of whom could sing or dance— which is quite a handicap if you're working on

ABOVE *The birth of Timothy Kelly in March 1962 brightened a rather dismal period in Gene's career. For him, as for Jeannie, the family now came first.* ☆

a musical with a star who, to tell the truth, could no longer sing or dance at anything like his previous peak. The American in Rochefort bore little resemblance to the American in Paris of sixteen years earlier.

By the end of 1967, Gene found himself back in California, depressed after half a dozen years of flops or aborted plans, both at home and abroad. As so often happens when you least expect it, he got the offer that would restore his fortunes and his self-confidence, at least as a director. *A Guide for the Married Man* was, on the face of it, just another all-star Hollywood sex comedy about the man of the title (Walter Matthau) going out for a series of abortive affairs before discovering that true love lies at home with Inger Stevens as his long-suffering wife. This plot had been tried many times before, but what Kelly did was to turn the joke on its head so that the philandering male, rather than the neglected wife, becomes the figure of fun. That, and a strong guest-star team (Lucille Ball, Jack Benny, Sid Caesar, Art Carney, Jayne Mansfield, Carl Reiner, Phil Silvers, and Terry-Thomas) turned what might have been a routine and indeed rather tasteless bedroom farce into a runaway hit, coming, as it did, at just the late-1960s moment when all marital (and indeed sexual) relationships were up for drastic re-evaluation.

Gene's triumph here with one of the biggest box-office hits of the year made him once again bankable and Darryl Zanuck even agreed to start work on one of Kelly's long-cherished projects, a semi-animated version of *Tom Sawyer*. There was, as usual, just one little snag. If Gene was to do this, he would also have to take on, as a favor to Zanuck and Fox, what proved to be one of the greatest high-budget disasters in the history of the Hollywood musical.

Because of its unexpected success five years earlier with *The Sound of Music*, Fox had now embroiled itself in the most costly mistake ever made by the American film industry. In rapid succession it had sunk $20 million into the Julie Andrews *Star*, then $18 million into the Rex Harrison *Doctor Dolittle*, and it was now about to invest a record-breaking $25 million in the Barbra Streisand *Hello, Dolly!*. Their total losses on these three pictures were enough to bring down not only the Fox studios but effectively the whole of old Hollywood.

None of this was yet clear, however, when Gene, somewhat reluctantly, began to set up *Hello, Dolly!*. Barbra Streisand had already been chosen, although not by Gene, over the obvious choice of Carol Channing, who had not only created the role on Broadway but was still to be found playing it there thirty years later to standing ovations. Fox had also

rejected such other stage Dollys as Mary Martin, Ginger Rogers, and Betty Grable; in going for Streisand, purely on the strength of her recent *Funny Girl* success, it effectively destroyed the whole point of Thornton Wilder's *The Matchmaker*, on which Jerry Herman's musical was based. This was that Dolly should be a warm-hearted older woman. Indeed, she had already been played like that on screen by Shirley Booth when the original play was filmed. Now, by playing Dolly as a young woman, Fox had changed the entire emphasis and the story became that of a gold-digger with an eye on the main chance.

The shooting was little short of a nightmare for all concerned. Streisand was at her most demanding and rapidly incurred the cordial loathing of her co-star, Walter Matthau, who, after one particular row, told her, first, to "stop directing the fucking picture," and second to remember that he was the actor on the set while she was merely a pipsqueak singer. As she departed for her dressing room in tears, he scored the final shot: "You don't have the talent of a butterfly's fart and although you may think you're indispensable, just remember that's what Betty Hutton thought." The following

morning Streisand began to get her own back, presenting Matthau with a bar of soap, "for your old sewermouth," and reminding him that the film was not in fact to be called *Hello, Walter!*

Gene was left on the sidelines of the set, watching these bust-ups with a mixture of amazement and irritation. His professionalism was hourly outraged and he was less than delighted to read an interview Streisand gave during filming in which she claimed that although Kelly was good at the geography of pictures, he had no idea at all about characterization.

As work went on in sweltering New York heat, with heavy period costumes and wigs often getting soaked by sudden storms, the mood on the film was dark and Kelly, though vastly better mannered than either of his stars, wanted, like them, to be anywhere other than there. Though he never went as far as Matthau, who described Barbra as "a freak attraction, like a boa constrictor," Gene found her insecurity and his irritability more than enough to destroy any of the pleasure there might have been in the filming of one of the greatest American musicals of the second half of the century.

LEFT *A welcome light moment during the shooting of* Hello, Dolly!, *which Gene directed. The mutual loathing of Barbra Streisand and Walter Matthau made the production a nightmare.* ☆

15. Who Could Ask for Anything More?

In exactly thirty Hollywood years, the one thing Gene had never done, on either side of the camera, was a western. And even that gap was filled, in 1969, when James Stewart and Henry Fonda brought him a script called *The Cheyenne Social Club* about two grizzled old cowboys running a bordello in Wyoming. A screenplay by James Lee Barrett did not aim much higher than portraying a kind of western "odd couple," but such was the charm of the two legendary old outdoorsmen and so subtle was Kelly's direction that they finished up with a delightful and nostalgic picture which, in its own quiet way, started the vogue for such late-life reunions as those of Fonda and Hepburn in *On Golden Pond* and Matthau and Lemmon as *Two Grumpy Old Men*. But even this picture, though vastly easier and happier than *Hello, Dolly!*, was underlined by sadness as James Stewart received the news that his stepson had been killed in Vietnam. The old pro kept on working, and he and Gene and Henry Fonda were to remain firm friends.

> *"When the definitive history of the Hollywood musical comes to be written, Gene Kelly will be seen as one of its heroes"*
>
> **DAVID SHIPMAN**

RIGHT *His last (and best) film as director:* The Cheyenne Social Club, *a mellow western starring James Stewart (left) and Henry Fonda (standing).* ☆

But Gene now realized that he could hardly make a living on the chance of an occasional directing gig or simply by turning up to say a few gracious words at the increasing number of retrospectives and Hollywood musical tributes that were now being organized almost annually in Los Angeles, New York, London, and Paris. Early in 1971 an answer seemed to present itself. Two young producers approached him with the idea of a mammoth mobile family show, modeled shamelessly on *Disney on Parade* but highlighted by a vast "Clown Machine" set designed by one of the most innovative of all designers and architects, Sean Kenny. This—50 feet wide and 130 feet long, weighing 44,000 pounds— could be raised above any stage or stadium to form itself into a vast mechanized series of ramps and rings, and was able to transform itself at the push of a button into jungles, ships, or fairgrounds. It was essentially, and way before its time, a kind of portable theme park. To a score by Moose Charlap (who, with Jules Styne, had written *Peter Pan* for Mary Martin), the new traveling circus show was to be called *Clownaround*. The plan was for Gene to choreograph and star. Tragically, however, on March 11th 1972, with *Clownaround* still at the audition stage, Gene received a phone call from Jeanne, who had just been to see her doctor for what they thought was a routine check-up. The doctor, she told Gene, had diagnosed leukemia and she could be dead in less than three weeks. In the event she was to live another fifteen months, and for most of that time the Kellys kept the news of her illness even from their children, let alone the always-inquisitive Hollywood press.

For a while Gene kept working on *Clownaround* and even opened it in Oakland, California. But when, as was perhaps inevitable given the fantastically ambitious nature of Sean Kenny's set, the entire show built around it collapsed in a welter of unpaid debts, Gene returned to Jeanne's bedside; he stayed there throughout her illness, never taking on work unless it was within a mile or two of his home. Indeed, apart from one-night cabaret and concert stands, the only work he did during these agonizing months of his beloved Jeanne's illness was six days on *Forty Carats*, the Paris, London, and Broadway stage hit which was now being filmed with Liv Ullmann and Eddie Albert. Gene gave an elegant performance as the ex-husband, and even agreed to do a little fast-tempo dancing with the veteran Binnie Barnes. "*Forty Carats* was for me an absolute luxury," he later reflected. "When you direct a film you have to shoot and edit, and that takes at least a year out of your life. As an actor you rehearse, play

ABOVE *Although Stewart suffered a personal tragedy during* The Cheyenne Social Club, *its making led to the three men remaining firm friends.* ☆

your scenes, collect your money, and are home by the end of the week."

The following year, 1973, was the worst of Gene's life. Within six months his indomitable mother, Harriet, died; and Noel Singer, his old friend and business manager, also went. Worst of all, Jeanne died on May 10th, 1973, as gracefully and thoughtfully as she had lived. "In her last three weeks," said her housekeeper, "she showed us exactly how to do everything for Gene and the children, exactly as she had always done it. She even told us which place-mats were to be used for which meals; just because she herself wasn't going to be around she saw no reason why the house should not be run as well as it always had been." In the next few months Gene, devastated by her death, took their two children back to Europe, first to meet those distant relatives he still had in Ireland, and then to London where Kerry, now married and following her career as a psychologist, had just given him his first grandchild.

Returning to California, resigned to the fact that Hollywood, already deeply into sex and violence, was no longer an industry in which he could expect to work, he devoted himself to fathering his still-young children. He refused to allow them to be brought up by nannies or turn them over to hired help; his priority for the entire time that they were at

home was to make sure that, unlike most movie stars, he was always there—even to supervise the homework.

He did work, of course, but now on a vast range of television specials, either as host or guest; in what had become an absolutely familiar format he would chat a little about the old days and then gently sing or dance one of his greatest hits. But in 1976, by which time he had made frequent appearances on Mary Tyler Moore's, Steve Lawrence's, and even the conjurer Doug Henning's weekly shows, an even better idea came along.

MGM, already in financial freefall, and therefore desperate to cash in what remaining assets could be found around the studio, suddenly realized it was sitting on vaults containing some of the greatest musicals ever made. Jack Haley Jr., a Hollywood brat whose father had been The Scarecrow in *The Wizard of Oz*, was now Director of Creative Affairs at Metro and, having already tried out one of the first television archive series, *Hollywood and the Stars*, he now saw no reason not to repeat the format on the wide screen, inviting surviving Golden Age stars to introduce excerpts from their own movies. From that simple idea, and from a growing sense of nostalgia for times past which was just beginning in the wider population, grew four highly profitable compilations: *That's*

Entertainment (1974), *That's Entertainment II* (1976), *That's Dancing* (1985), and the only one in which Gene was not actively involved, *That's Entertainment III* (1994). These epic anthologies were not immediately hits at the box office but happily they coincided with the coming of the commercial videotape and consequently sold in their millions to home viewers anxious to build up their libraries without having to sit through "the boring bits."

The best of these, certainly from Gene's point of view, was *That's Entertainment II*, for which he and Fred Astaire were co-hosts. Gene was also the director of the new sequences and was therefore able to devise for himself (now sixty-four) and Fred (seventy-seven) their final screen dances. For so many years they had been compared. Now they were together with nothing at all to prove. They sang, they danced, they joked—and it was magic.

All the positive and negative comments made about them over a span of half a century didn't matter except to add piquancy. Dilys Powell quipped: "Astaire for elegance, Kelly for command," while a young film student at UCLA wrote: "A woman might give her heart and soul to Fred Astaire but she saves her body for Gene Kelly." *Picturegoer* moaned about Gene: "His career is notable for an absolute absence of scandal. None of the 'Inside Hollywood' columns ever managed to get anything on him at all. He was as squeaky clean as Fred Astaire." They were, separately and together, just wonderful. This was the first time that Gene and Fred had shared a routine since "The Babbitt and the Bromide" in *Ziegfeld Follies* exactly thirty years earlier and when they danced off together hand in hand toward the final closing titles what they were subliminally giving us was one final message: MGM might now have an extremely dubious future but it had sure had one hell of a past.

From that, however, Gene went on to make, in rapid succession, two of the worst films in which even he, growing increasingly careless, had ever been involved. The first of these, *Viva Knievel* (1977), was a ramshackle vehicle for the eponymous daredevil motorcyclist, with Gene cast as Evel's mentor in a role he later promised he had only accepted on behalf of his now teenaged kids, both then fascinated by motorbikes. The second was his last and worst ever movie musical. At sixty-eight he somehow got himself caught in *Xanadu*, a surrealist attempt to relocate the old Hollywood classic musicals in a setting of MTV. For original Kelly buffs the in-joke here was that Gene's character had the same name, Danny McGuire, as the character he had played opposite Rita Hayworth in

Cover Girl, but like the rest of the film this joke is never explained and leads to nothing. In one or two moments, Gene sings and dances (once even on roller skates) with Olivia Newton-John and it is just possible to see in their duet, "Whenever You're Away From Me," something of what this film could have been if anybody had really bothered to write, direct, or choreograph it. Aside from the MGM anthologies, this was Gene's very last feature film as singer-dancer-actor and it is simply awful to realize that he went out on that title. Gene agreed. "I have to admit that was a simply terrible picture. It could have been made in a third of the time at a third of the cost but nobody had the faintest idea what they were doing and it showed me how depressingly little today's crop of youngsters actually know about making musicals."

However, there were consolations. Throughout the 1980s he was still very active in television and as the children grew to college age he felt more and more able to leave them for concert tours. He also, for the first time in almost half a century, rediscovered the delights of appearing in stage plays and musicals. As early as 1974 he had done a season of *Take Me Along* in summer stock and his dream now was to direct a full Broadway staging of a new musical life of Louis Armstrong, to be called *Satchmo*. He and

David Niven Jr. (his producer on *That's Dancing* and *That's Entertainment II*) were, at the same time, trying to set up a movie musical life of Santa Claus. Both these projects, after many months of pre-production work, floundered when the budgets could not be raised.

Even Gene now admitted he was too old to give up another year or two of his life to apparently impossible dreams. Instead, he then spent much of his time traveling around Europe and America, picking up all the honors that were being showered on him as if by way of apology for the fact that nobody could find him any real work. After the Legion of Honor and the Kennedy Center Award came one of the best tributes that Gene ever received, this one the highest accolade that can be given by Hollywood: the Lifetime Achievement Award of the American Film Institute. It was then and there that Yves Montand, with whom Gene had briefly danced in *Let's Make Love*, declared: "Gene put dance on the street. For the first time, we saw a classical dancer in trousers, a short shirt and loafers, yet still elegant, dancing on the sidewalk, and making us feel that any of us could dance just like him. Gene will always be our American in Paris."

London, keen to get in on the Gene Kelly honors act, promptly invited him to host a

Royal Command Performance, and it was with such memorable one-off events that Gene was to mark the last ten years of his otherwise uneventful professional life.

In private he was now living the life of an aging widower, happy enough to play host to his few surviving close friends and of course to the kids whenever they came home from college. Mercifully, both were home for Christmas when, on the night of December 22nd, 1983, fire broke out in his beloved two-storey home, the one that he and Betsy had bought shortly after his return to Hollywood immediately after the war. His son Tim dragged him from the burning house, and although no one was injured the fire that gutted the building took with it a lifetime's priceless collection of trophies, awards, photographs, art, and personal memories. Most of these proved irreplaceable (Boston University has the only surviving collection of Kelly memorabilia) but Gene himself was characteristically reserved and resilient about a disaster which might have destroyed many other seventy year olds. "What will you do?" inquired one of the many reporters who rang him in the hotel to which the family had been forced to decamp in their pajamas. "Rebuild, of course," replied Gene, and that was precisely what he did. Within a year, a new house had risen from the ashes, this time a state-of-the-art mansion with five bedrooms and six bathrooms, and it was there that Gene was to live out the last decade of his life.

But he still had one great surprise left. Gene had often been asked to write his autobiography but had pleaded a number of excuses. He was too busy, or he couldn't find his notes, or (from 1984 on) he had lost the necessary documents in the fire. Finally he hired a young journalist, Patricia Ward, to help him. Within a few weeks she was living on his property in the poolhouse and although she was fifty years younger, a close, not to say intimate, alliance was quickly forged. In 1990, at a ceremony in Santa Barbara boycotted by all three of his children, Gene Kelly married his third wife, Patricia.

By all contemporary Hollywood accounts it was not an easy late-life marriage; soon after the wedding Gene bought his twenty-seven-year-old bride her own house and BMW sports car, a gesture which deeply irritated those of his remaining circle who had always found him habitually tightfisted. The rumors around Hollywood were that Gene and Patricia had quickly reached a post-nuptial settlement. They would live reasonably separate lives under different roofs, but she would always be available to accompany him to the many public functions at which he still found recognition, acclaim, and a few old friends.

But he was still open to offers. One of the last and, on the face of it, most attractive, came from the director Francis Ford Coppola who, riding high on the success of his *Godfather* sequence, set up Zoetrope as a studio with the unusual brief of bringing together all that was best in Hollywood's past and present. The idea was that Gene should recruit for Coppola a production staff to rival the old Freed unit at MGM. "I was over the moon with joy and expectation," Gene said. "This looked like the plum job of all time as well as the best and most effective and exciting way to pass on everything I had ever learned from the day I had arrived at MGM in 1941."

Money was to be no object and the first production would be a musical called *One from the Heart* starring Frederic Forrest, Nastassia Kinski and Harry Dean Stanton. It was not, to put it mildly, a success. "If this is the essence of cinema," said Dilys Powell in *The Sunday Times*, "then Salvador Dali is the essence of painting." In the end, Gene's only real contribution was to assist the choreographer, Kenny Ortega, through a couple of the routines, and the disastrous failure of the movie brought down the entire Zoetrope edifice. "Sadly," said Gene, "Coppola simply over-extended himself. He just didn't have the money to capitalize all those grandiose dreams."

On a happier note, in 1994 President Clinton presented Gene with the National Medal of the Arts.

But of all the plaudits that were now pouring in, the one that perhaps meant most to him was a remarkable 5,000-word essay written by the novelist John Updike in the *New Yorker*, on Gene's eighty-first birthday in 1994. He concluded: "To the question 'How can I get a guy/girl?' the Hollywood musicals answered, 'Dance with/sing to him/her' ... around 1955 they began to melt away. The profitable movie musicals to follow will tend to feature Elvis Presley. The tune changed— rock and roll (its very name gutsy and lewd) made the elaborate sublimations of the musical comedy seem arcane, if not silly. Another language had become academic. Few spoke the language when it was a live one with more fluency than Gene Kelly, and none more thrillingly embodied American élan."

Well into the early 1990s and his own early eighties, Gene continued to make frequent, albeit increasingly frail, public appearances at banquets and fundraisers, and would even give the occasional movie lecture to students at the nearby University of Southern California. But the deaths in these years of such friends as the agent Swifty Lazar and the director Richard Brooks, coupled with his own mild stroke in February 1995, were bringing

ABOVE *Gene takes a break during the shooting of the* Young Girls of Rochefort, *for once apparently feeling his years.* ☆

Gene up against intimations of his own mortality. He knew that he had now lived long enough to establish his professional immortality and, as if to prove this, when in the last year of his life GAP used classic photographs from the 1940s and 1950s to advertise a new range of khaki jeans. Gene and Arthur Miller were the only two living people in a campaign which otherwise starred Marilyn Monroe, Ernest Hemingway, and Amelia Earhart. Although he had been doing more and more television ads, Gene claimed that this one gave him the greatest pleasure. "This has real class."

By now, more and more critics and historians were starting to celebrate *Singin' in the Rain*. As Peter Wollen has noted in his brilliant 1992 monograph on *Singin' in the Rain* for the British Film Institute, the musical had originally taken a long time to get established, not least because it was pulled back soon after first release so that *An American in Paris*, which had just won several Oscars, could be re-released in its place. But over the years its popularity grew and by 1982 it had made fourth place in the *Sight & Sound* international critics' poll of the best movies of all time (beaten only by *Citizen Kane, La Règle du Jeu* and *The Seven Samurai*). There were few film historians alert enough to realize that the classic title dance in the puddles was a solo reprise of the number that Kelly, Phil Silvers and Rita Hayworth had done as "Make Way For Tomorrow" in the 1944 *Cover Girl*, complete with doorway-ducking and disapproving street cop.

The other big number "Make 'Em Laugh," had been more a matter of luck than judgment, as Donald O'Connor later recalled: "Gene didn't have a clue as to what kind of number it was supposed to be: we just went into the rehearsal room and came up with a compendium of gags and 'shtick' that I had done since my earliest vaudeville days. Every time I got to something that was good or worked for me, Gene would write it down and bit by bit the whole number was constructed."

It was eighteen months after *Singin' in the Rain* was completed that Gene realized what a triumph he had scored, when he was taken by Jule Styne to watch the Coronation procession of Queen Elizabeth II. As he later noted with pride: "Over the loudspeaker system a man who had been keeping everyone informed of what was happening said: 'And now, ladies and gentlemen, I'd like you all to join Gene Kelly in "Singin' in the Rain,"' and on came the record. Seconds later, thousands of lovely, cold, wet, shivering English men and women started to sing. It was the biggest thrill of my entire life. It beat anything I'd ever known: the opening night of *Pal Joey*, my Academy

ABOVE *Gene, aged seventy, with his children, Bridget, Timothy and Kerry.* ☆

Award, you name it. It was a once-in-a-lifetime experience, and I felt if I never achieved another thing, which was the way things seemed to be going at the time. I had justified my existence. Suddenly and for the rest of my life the English could do no wrong."

The Americans could, however: there are now very real grounds for suggesting that Kelly's apparently aberrant decision to move to Europe at the height of his Hollywood career was not only for reasons of taxation or his wife's politics. Kelly, too, had been involved with the unions and considerably harrassed for mixing with the hated "left-wing circles" of these scoundrel years. Growing up in steel-industry Pittsburgh during the Depression had made him a natural socialist, and although he was always more careful than his wife to keep his political allegiances to himself, there was already such a thing as guilt by association: Adolph Green, co-writer of *Singin' in the Rain*, had already been denounced as a Communist, as had one of his cabaret partners, Judy Holliday. As the witch-hunt years dragged on Kelly had to come to the rescue of Mrs Kelly when she was about to lose her great role in *Marty* on political grounds. In the midst of filming *It's Always Fair Weather*, Kelly stormed into Dore Schary's office and issued an ultimatum: either her name was removed from the blacklist or he would leave the studio for ever. Schary knew he was beaten, and Betsy Blair got to make *Marty*.

In the light of all this, as Wollen has observed, it is possible with the wisdom of hindsight to read all kinds of messages into the apparently innocuous screenplay of *Singin' in the Rain*. The plot, after all, hinges upon a greedy studio chief's attempt to "blacklist" Kathy Selden, and even the title dance sequence could be interpreted as Kelly being resolutely cheerful in a miserable climate, whether political or meteorological, insisting that although unorthodox, he is at the end of the day just another law-abiding American bowing before the law of a street cop.

Others have been keen to point out that *Singin' in the Rain* is just a variant on Hans Andersen's *Little Match Girl*, in which the heroine's voice is stolen by a wicked witch (Lina Lamont) but is restored in time for her to marry her Prince Charming (Kelly). Cinderella is in there somewhere too; and those who don't believe in fiction might want to recall that Kelly's father had been a phonograph record traveling salesman put out of work by the Wall Street Crash and then by the revolution that radio and talking pictures brought to the gramophone industry. If *Singin' in the Rain* is about anything serious, it is surely about the devastating impact of a new technology on old-established working practices.

Still one more theme of the picture is the importance of keeping a trio alive, one that runs through many of the Kelly musicals all the way back to *On the Town*; Gene, it may be recalled, only went solo after starting out in a triple-act with Fred and their sister Louise, one that then became the double-act of Fred and Gene before Gene alone went on to stardom. Most psychiatrists would be able to read something about sibling guilt into all of that.

Gene's last major appearance, give or take a few more industry banquets and fund-raisers, was on July 16th, 1994, when an audience of millions all over the world saw him take a bow at a Three Tenors concert at Dodger Stadium during which Domingo, Carreras and Pavarotti had, with much goodwill but surprisingly little understanding, belted out Gene's "Singin' in the Rain." We were not to know that his gracious farewell wave to them was also meant for us. After two more minor strokes, Gene Kelly, the exuberant, charismatic hoofer who danced and sang and smiled and splashed his way into the hearts of three generations, died peacefully in his sleep on February 2nd, 1996. He was eighty-three. His wife Patricia was at his bedside.

Stations worldwide ran entire weeks of his movies, tributes were paid by all surviving co-stars and although the funeral was private, the mourning was universal. The public outpouring of affection was immediate and longlasting. In private an ugly rift opened between Gene's third wife and his three children by Betsy and Jeanne over the terms of his will, but none of that concerns a world audience who want to remember the man who took dancing out of white tie and tails and set it bubbling on the furnace of street life.

This was the man who had made twelve musicals for Arthur Freed at MGM, of which six were co-choreographed or co-directed by Stanley Donen. This was the man who introduced such hit songs as "Long Ago and Far Away" and "Be a Clown;" the man who danced romantically with Judy Garland, with Cyd Charisse, Kathryn Grayson, and Vera-Ellen as well as Rita Hayworth, Esther Williams, Leslie Caron, Debbie Reynolds, Mitzi Gaynor, and Shirley MacLaine; the man who danced with Frank Sinatra, Fred Astaire and with Jerry Mouse and Donald O'Connor —all unforgettably.

This was the boy from Pittsburgh who turned his face up to the streetlight and taught us what it meant to sing and dance for the sheer joy of ignoring the elements. He wasn't a legend—he was Gene Kelly.

Filmography

FOR ME AND MY GAL (1942) MGM
Produced by Arthur Freed, *directed by* Busby Berkeley.
Judy Garland, Gene Kelly, George Murphy, Marta Eggerth,
Ben Blue, Lucille Norman, Richard Quine, Keenan Wynn,
Horace McNally.

PILOT NUMBER 5 (1943) MGM
Produced by B.P. Fineman, *directed by* George Sidney.
Franchot Tone, Marsha Hunt, Gene Kelly, Van Johnson, Dick
Simmons, Steve Geray, Howard Freeman, Frank Puglia.

DUBARRY WAS A LADY (1943) MGM
Produced by Arthur Freed, *directed by* Roy del Ruth.
Red Skelton, Lucille Ball, Gene Kelly, Virginia O'Brien, Rags
Ragland, Zero Mostel, Donald Meek, Douglas Dumbrille.

THOUSANDS CHEER (1943) MGM
Produced by Joe Pasternak, *directed by* George Sidney.
Kathryn Grayson, Gene Kelly, Mary Astor, John Boles, Ben
Blue, Frances Rafferty, Mary Elliott.
guest stars: Mickey Rooney, Judy Garland, Red Skelton,
Eleanor Powell, Ann Sothern, Virginia O'Brien, Lucille Ball,
Lena Horne, Marsha Hunt, Frank Morgan, Marilyn Maxwell,
Donna Reed, June Allyson, Gloria de Haven, Margaret
O'Brien, John Conte, Sara Haden, José Iturbi, Don Loper and
Maxine Barrat, Kay Kyser, Bob Crosby and Benny Carter and
their bands.

THE CROSS OF LORRAINE (1943) MGM
Produced by Edwin Knopf, *directed by* Tay Garnett.
Jean-Pierre Aumont, Gene Kelly, Sir Cedric Hardwicke,
Richard Whorf, Joseph Calleia, Peter Lorre, Hume Cronyn,
Billy Roy, Tonio Stewart, Jack Lambert, Wallace Ford,
Donald Curtis, Jack Edwards Jr., Richard Ryen.

COVER GIRL (1944) COLUMBIA
Produced by Arthur Schwartz, *directed by* Charles Vidor.
Rita Hayworth, Gene Kelly, Lee Bowman, Phil Silvers, Jinx
Falkenburg, Leslie Brooks, Eve Arden, Otto Kruger, Jess
Barker, Curt Bois, Ed Brophy, Thurston Hall.

CHRISTMAS HOLIDAY (1944) UNIVERSAL
Produced by Felix Jackson, *directed by* Robert Siodmak.
Deanna Durbin, Gene Kelly, Richard Whorf, Dean Harens,
Gale Sondergaard, Gladys George, David Bruce.

ANCHORS AWEIGH (1945) MGM
Produced by Joe Pasternak, *directed by* George Sidney.
Frank Sinatra, Kathryn Grayson, Gene Kelly, José Iturbi,
Dean Stockwell, Pamela Britton, Rags Ragland, Billy Gilbert,
Edgar Kennedy, Henry O'Neill, Carlos Ramirez, Grady
Sutton, Leon Ames, Sharon McManus.

ZIEGFELD FOLLIES (1946) MGM
Produced by Arthur Freed, *directed by* Vincente Minnelli.
Fred Astaire, Lucille Ball, Lucille Bremer, Fanny Brice, Judy
Garland, Kathryn Grayson, Lena Horne, Gene Kelly, James
Melton, Victor Moore, Red Skelton, Esther Williams, William
Powell, Edward Arnold, Marion Bell, Cyd Charisse, Hume
Cronyn, William Frawley, Robert Lewis, Virginia O'Brien,
Keenan Wynn.

LIVING IN A BIG WAY (1947) MGM
Produced by Pandro S. Berman, *directed by* Gregory LaCava.
Gene Kelly, Marie McDonald, Charles Winniger, Phyllis
Thaxter, Spring Byington, Jean Adair, Clinton Sundberg,
John Warburton.

THE PIRATE (1948) MGM
Produced by Arthur Freed, *directed by* Vincente Minnelli.
Judy Garland, Gene Kelly, Walter Slezak, Gladys Cooper,
Reginald Owen, George Zucco, The Nicholas Brothers, Lester
Allen, Lola Deem.

THE THREE MUSKETEERS (1948) MGM
Produced by Pandro S. Berman, *directed by* George Sidney.
Lana Turner, Gene Kelly, June Allyson, Angela Lansbury, Van
Heflin, Frank Morgan, Vincent Price, Keenan Wynn, John
Sutton, Gig Young, Robert Coote, Reginald Owen, Ian Keith,
Patricia Medina, Richard Stapley.

WORDS AND MUSIC (1948) MGM
Produced by Arthur Freed, *directed by* Norman Taurog.
Mickey Rooney, Tom Drake, Marshall Thompson, Janet Leigh, Betty Garrett, Ann Sothern, Perry Como, Jeanette Nolan, Clinton Sundberg, Harry Antrim, Richard Quine, Ilka Gruning, Emory Parnell.
guest stars: Gene Kelly, Vera-Ellen, Judy Garland, Lena Horne, Cyd Charisse, Mel Tormé, Dee Turnell, The Blackburn Twins, Allyn McLerie.

TAKE ME OUT TO THE BALL GAME
(EVERYBODY'S CHEERING) (1949) MGM
Produced by Arthur Freed, *directed by* Busby Berkeley.
Frank Sinatra, Esther Williams, Gene Kelly, Betty Garrett, Edward Arnold, Jules Munshin, Richard Lane, Tom Dugan, Saul Gorss, Douglas Fowley, Eddie Parkes, James Burke.

ON THE TOWN (1950) MGM
Produced by Arthur Freed, *directed by* Gene Kelly and Stanley Donen.
Gene Kelly, Frank Sinatra, Betty Garrett, Ann Miller, Jules Munshin, Vera-Ellen, Florence Bates, Alice Pearce, George Meader.

THE BLACK HAND (1950) MGM
Produced by William H. Wright, *directed by* Richard Thorpe.
Gene Kelly, J. Carrol Naish, Teresa Celli, Marc Lawrence, Frank Puglia, Barry Kelly, Mario Siletti, Peter Brocco.

SUMMER STOCK (1950) MGM
Produced by Joe Pasternak, *directed by* Charles Walters.
Judy Garland, Gene Kelly, Eddie Bracken, Gloria de Haven, Marjorie Main, Phil Silvers, Ray Collins, Nita Bieber, Carleton Carpenter, Hans Conreid.

AN AMERICAN IN PARIS (1951) MGM
Produced by Arthur Freed, *directed by* Vincente Minnelli.
Gene Kelly, Leslie Caron, Oscar Levant, Georges Guetary, Nina Foch, Martha Bamattre, Anna Q. Nilsson.

IT'S A BIG COUNTRY (1952) MGM
Produced by Robert Sisk, *directed by* Richard Thorpe, John Sturges, Charles Vidor, Don Weis, Clarence Brown, William Wellman, Don Hartman.
Ethel Barrymore, Gary Cooper, Van Johnson, Gene Kelly, Janet Leigh, Fredric March, William Powell, S.Z. Sakall, Marjorie Main, George Murphy, Keefe Brasselle, James Whitmore, Keenan Wynn, Nancy Davis, Lewis Stone, Leon Ames.

SINGIN' IN THE RAIN (1952) MGM
Produced by Arthur Freed, *directed by* Gene Kelly and Stanley Donen.
Gene Kelly, Donald O'Connor, Debbie Reynolds, Jean Hagen, Millard Mitchell, Rita Moreno, Douglas Fowley, Cyd Charisse, Madge Black, King Donovan, Kathleen Freeman, Bobby Watson, Tommy Farrell.

THE DEVIL MAKES THREE (1952) MGM
Produced by Richard Goldstone, *directed by* Andrew Marton.
Gene Kelly, Pier Angeli, Richard Rober, Richard Egan, Claus Clausen, Wilfred Seyferth, Margot Hielscher, Annie Rosar, Harold Benedict.

INVITATION TO THE DANCE (1956) MGM
Produced by Arthur Freed, *directed by* Gene Kelly.
Igor Youskevitch, Claire Sombert, Gene Kelly, Carol Haney, David Kasday, Irving Davies, Tamara Toumanova, Tommy Rawl, Claude Bessy, Belita, Diane Adams, Daphne Dalle, David Paltenghi.

CREST OF THE WAVE (SEAGULLS OVER SORRENTO) (1954) MGM
Produced and directed by John and Roy Boulting.
Gene Kelly, John Justin, Bernard Lee, Jeff Richards, Sidney James, Patrick Doonan, Ray Jackson, Fred Wayne, Patrick Barr, David Orr.

BRIGADOON (1954) MGM
Produced by Arthur Freed, *directed by* Vincente Minnelli.
Gene Kelly, Van Johnson, Cyd Charisse, Elaine Stwart, Barry Jones, Hugh Laing, Albert Sharpe, Virginia Bosier, Jimmy Thompson.

In a Greenwich Village honky-tonk, Gene Kelly meets Cyd Charisse and goes for her in a big way while her gangster friends are not amused.

DEEP IN MY HEART (1955) MGM
Produced by Roger Edens, *directed by* Stanley Donen.
José Ferrer, Merle Oberon, Helen Traubel, Doe Avedon, Walter Pidgeon, Paul Henreid, Tamara Toumanova, Paul Stewart, Isobel Elsom, Douglas Fowley, Russ Tamblyn. *guest stars*: Rosemary Clooney, Gene and Fred Kelly, Jane Powell, Vic Damone, Ann Miller, William Olvis, Cyd Charisse, James Mitchell, Howard Keel, Tony Martin, Joan Weldon.

IT'S ALWAYS FAIR WEATHER (1955) MGM
Produced by Arthur Freed, *directed by* Gene Kelly and Stanley Donen.
Gene Kelly, Dan Dailey, Cyd Charisse, Dolores Gray, Michael Kidd, David Burns, Jay C. Flippen, Hal March.

THE HAPPY ROAD (1957) RELEASED BY MGM
Produced and directed by Gene Kelly.
Gene Kelly, Barbara Laage, Bobby Clark, Brigitte Fossey, Roger Treville, Jess Hahn, Maryse Martin, Michael Redgrave, Van Doude.

LES GIRLS (1957) MGM
Produced by Sol C. Siegel, *directed by* George Cukor.
Gene Kelly, Mitzi Gaynor, Kay Kendall, Taina Elg, Jacques Bergerac, Leslie Phillips, Henry Daniell, Patrick MacNee, Stephen Vercoe.

THE TUNNEL OF LOVE (1958) MGM
Produced by Joseph Fields and Martin Melcher, *directed by* Gene Kelly.
Doris Day, Richard Widmark, Gig Young, Gia Scala, Elizabeth Fraser, Elizabeth Wilson, Vikki Dougan, Doodles Weaver.

MARJORIE MORNINGSTAR (1958) WARNER BROS.
Produced by Milton Sperling, *directed by* Irving Rapper.
Gene Kelly, Natalie Wood, Claire Trevor, Ed Wynn, Everett Sloane, Marty Milner, Carolyn Jones, Martin Balsam, Jesse White, Edward Byrnes.

INHERIT THE WIND (1960) UNITED ARTISTS
Produced and directed by Stanley Kramer.
Spencer Tracy, Frederic March, Gene Kelly, Florence Eldridge, Dick York, Donna Anderson, Harry Morgan, Elliott Reid, Philip Coolidge, Claude Akins, Paul Hartman, Jimmy Boyd.

LET'S MAKE LOVE (1960) 20TH CENTURY-FOX
Produced by Jerry Wald, *directed by* George Cukor.
Marilyn Monroe, Yves Montand, Tony Randall, Frankie Vaughan, Wilfrid Hyde-White, David Burns, Michael David. *guest stars*: Milton Berle, Bing Crosby, Gene Kelly.

GIGOT (1962)
SEVEN ARTS PRODUCTION RELEASED BY 20TH CENTURY-FOX.
Produced by Kenneth Hyman, *directed by* Gene Kelly.
Jackie Gleason, Katherine Kath, Gabrielle Dorziat, Jean Lefebvre, Jacques Marin, Albert Rémy, Yvonne Constant, Germaine Delbat.

WHAT A WAY TO GO (1964)
RELEASED BY 20TH CENTURY-FOX
Produced by Arthur P. Jacobs, *directed by* J. Lee Thompson.
Shirley MacLaine, Paul Newman, Robert Mitchum, Dean Martin, Gene Kelly, Bob Cummings, Dick Van Dyke, Reginald Gardiner, Margaret Dumont, Lou Nova, Fifi D'Orsay, Maurice Marsac, Wally Vernon, Jane Wald, Lenny Kent.

THE YOUNG GIRLS OF ROCHEFORT (1968)
WARNER BROS. RELEASE
Produced by Mag Bodard, *directed by* Jacques Demy.
Catherine Deneuve, Françoise Dorléac, George Chakiris, Grover Dale, Gene Kelly, Danielle Darrieux, Jacques Perrin, Michel Piccoli.

A GUIDE FOR THE MARRIED MAN (1967)
20TH CENTURY-FOX.
Produced by Frank McCarthy, *directed by* Gene Kelly.
Walter Matthau, Robert Morse, Inger Stevens, Sue Ann
Langdon, Claire Kelly, Linda Harrison, Elaine Devry.
guest stars: Lucille Ball, Jack Benny, Polly Bergen, Joey
Bishop, Ben Blue, Sid Caesar, Art Carney, Wally Cox, Marty
Ingels, Ann Morgan Guilbert, Jeffrey Hunter, Sam Jaffe, Jayne
Mansfield, Hal March, Louis Nye, Carl Reiner, Phil Silvers,
Terry-Thomas.

HELLO, DOLLY! (1969) 20TH CENTURY-FOX
Produced by Ernest Lehman, *directed by* Gene Kelly.
Barbra Streisand, Walter Matthau, Michael Crawford, Louis
Armstrong, Marianne McAndrew, E.J. Peaker, Danny Lockin,
Joyce Ames, Tommy Tune, Judy Knaiz.

THE CHEYENNE SOCIAL CLUB (1970)
A NATIONAL GENERAL PRODUCTION
Produced and directed by Gene Kelly.
James Stewart, Henry Fonda, Shirley Jones, Sue Ann
Langdon, Dabbs Greer, Elaine Devry, Robert Middleston, Arc
Johnson, Jackie Russell.

FORTY CARATS (1973) COLUMBIA
Produced by Mike Frankovich, *directed by* Milton Katsclas.
Liv Ullmann, Edward Albert, Gene Kelly, Binnie Barnes,
Deborah Raffin, Billy Green Bush, Nancy Walker, Don Porter,
Rosemary Murphy.

THAT'S ENTERTAINMENT (1974) MGM
Produced by Jack Haley Jr.
Narrated by Fred Astaire, Gene Kelly, Liza Minnelli, Bing
Crosby, Peter Lawford, Donald O'Connor, Debbie Reynolds,
Mickey Rooney, Frank Sinatra, James Stewart, Elizabeth
Taylor.

THAT'S ENTERTAINMENT II (1976) MGM
Produced by Saul Chaplin and Daniel Melnick.
Narrated by Gene Kelly and Fred Astaire.

VIVA KNIEVEL (1977) WARNER BROS.
Produced by Stan Hough, *directed by* Gordon Douglas.

Evel Knievel, Gene Kelly, Red Buttons, Lauren Hutton, Leslie
Nielsen, Frank Gifford, Eric Olson, Sheila Allen, Cameron
Mitchell, Marjoe Gortner.

XANADU (1980) UNIVERSAL
Produced by Lawrence Gordon, *directed by* Robert Greenwald.
Olivia Newton-John, Michael Beck, Gene Kelly, Sandra Katie
Hanley, Fred McCarren, Ron Woods, Coral Browne, Wilfrid
Hyde-White.

THAT'S DANCING (1985) MGM
Produced by Jack Haley Jr. and David Niven Jr..
Executive Producer Gene Kelly.
Written and directed by Jack Haley Jr..

Television

1955–90: Countless appearances in musical specials.
1962: Series: *Going My Way*

Stage

1934–7: College and summer stock shows (amateur).
1938: *Hold Your Hats* (Pittsburgh Playhouse: dancer and
choreographer).
Leave it to Me (Imperial Theater, Broadway: feature role
and assistant choreographer).
One for the Money (Broadway: lead role and assistant
choreographer).
1939: *The Emperor Jones* (Westport, Connecticut:
choreographer).
The Time of Your Life (Booth, Broadway: Harry).
Green Grow the Lilacs (Westport, Connecticut:
choreographer).
The Magazine Page (Westport, Connecticut: master of
ceremonies).
Billy Rose's Diamond Horseshoe (Broadway: dance director).
Pal Joey (Ethel Barrymore Theater, New York: Joey Evans).
1941: *Best Foot Forward* (Broadway: choreographer).
1958: *The Flower Drum Song* (Broadway: director).
1974: *Take Me Along* (summer stock season).

Index

Acknowledgements

First and foremost, the authors wish to thank their drama-critic colleague and friend Clive Hirschhorn for so generously making available to them not only his 1974 (revised 1984) biography of Gene Kelly, the only one of its kind, but also his unrivaled knowledge of the Hollywood movie musical in Gene's time. We are also of course deeply grateful to Leslie Caron for her enchanting foreword.

We would like to thank too Graham Pass and Philip Glassborow for making their 1996 BBC Radio 2 documentary available to us, and Rosie Alison for showing us an interview she recorded with Gene for American television very close to the end of his life.

No book of this nature would be possible without the resources of the BBC, BFI, Lincoln Center and the Hollywood Academy of Motion Picture Arts and Sciences reference libraries; at this last address we would especially like to thank Sandra Archer for her unfailing assistance and hospitality on this as so many earlier biographies. Thanks also to everyone we have quoted here in print or direct speech, and apologies to those we have had to leave out for reasons of space.

Aquarius Library
Corbis UK
Kobal Collection
Photofest NY
Pictorial Press
Rex Features
© Bob Willoughby 1996

BFI Stills, Posters and Designs
with acknowledgement to:
Apjac/Orchard/20th Century-Fox, Columbia
Pictures, Metro-Goldwyn-Mayer, National General,
20th Century-Fox/Chenault.

OTHER BOOKS BY THE AUTHORS

Also by Ruth Leon:
The Applause Guide to the Performing Arts in New York

Also by Sheridan Morley:
A Talent to Amuse (the first biography of Noël Coward)
Review Copies: London Theatres 1970–74
Marlene Dietrich
Oscar Wilde
Sybil Thorndike: A Life in the Theatre
Gertrude Lawrence: A Bright Particular Star
Gladys Cooper
Tales from the Hollywood Raj: The British in California
Shooting Stars: London Theatres 1975–83
Katharine Hepburn
The Other Side of the Moon (the first biography of David Niven)
Spread a Little Happiness: The First 100 Years of the British Musical
Elizabeth Taylor
Odd Man Out (the first biography of James Mason)
Our Theatres in the Eighties: London Theatres 1983–89
Audrey Hepburn
Robert My Father
Ginger Rogers
Rank Outsider: The Career of Dirk Bogarde

and as editor:
The Noël Coward Diaries (with Graham Payn)
Noël Coward and his Friends (with Graham Payn and Cole Lesley)
Theatre 71, 72, 73, 74
The Theatre Addict's Archive
The Autobiographies of Noël Coward
Punch at the Theatre
The Stephen Sondheim Songbook
The Theatregoer's Quiz Book
Bull's Eyes (the memoirs of Peter Bull)
Out in the Midday Sun (the paintings of Noël Coward)
The Methuen Book of Theatrical Short Stories
The Methuen Book of Film Stories

for the stage:
Noël and Gertie: Spread A Little Happiness: Before the Fringe